WORSHIP FOR
EVERYONE

Nick and **Becky Drake** are widely recognised as leading practitioners and songwriters in the area of all-age worship. They have run Worship for Everyone as a ministry for over ten years, releasing a number of albums as well as running national conferences and training. They worship at Gas Street Church, where Nick is associate vicar.

Becky had a successful career in communications and PR in London before moving to Birmingham, where she now works as a school chaplain. She continues to lead worship and write songs under the Worship for Everyone banner. Nick is the author of *A Deeper Note* (Grove Books); is co-author of *Why Worship?*, the Spring Harvest book for 2021 (SPCK); and also teaches on worship through Worship Central and St Mellitus College, a training seminary for the Church of England. He recently completed his PhD in worship studies.

WORSHIP FOR EVERYONE

Nick Drake
and
Becky Drake

First published in Great Britain in 2021

Society for Promoting Christian Knowledge
36 Causton Street
London SW1P 4ST
www.spck.org.uk

British Library Cataloguing-in-Publication Data
A catalogue record for this book is available from the British Library

ISBN 978–0–281–08587–3
eBook ISBN 978–0–281–08588–0

1 3 5 7 9 10 8 6 4 2

Typeset by Westchester Publishing Services
Printed and bound in Great Britain by Ashford Colour Press

eBook by Westchester Publishing Services

Produced on paper from sustainable forests

Contents

Introduction

If there were a treasure—something good, something with tremendous power—that had been hidden, perhaps lost a long time ago and now forgotten about, would you not want to unearth it? Blow off the dust from it, and give it room to let its power be displayed once again?

Churches hunt and pursue many things—from comfortable seating to excellence in music, from dynamic preaching to beauty in sacrament—but what if they had forgotten to put prayer, time, energy and resource into one of the very basics, something right under their noses all along, something that has huge impact because of the unity it displays that echoes God's heart, something that should have a natural home in the church?

This book is about this long-lost treasure and how to nurture, pursue and facilitate it for your church. It's about the hidden power of generational diversity in worship, what we call simply 'Worship for Everyone'. Our society has become very good at separating people and pandering to individuals according to their ages and stages of life;[1] but the church should be a place where children and adults come together to be *one people,* experiencing together the promises, power and presence of God. In this special place where young and old gather, the unique power of unity across ages, generational diversity, is unleashed.

There was an article recently that spoke of this secret and described a hint of what can happen when this hidden power is released.[2] It was exploring the idea of bringing together children and the elderly in 'intergenerational care centres' across the UK. The article went on to say: 'Twinning nurseries with care homes for the elderly would boost children's reading and social skills ... [and] by playing and reading with children, the elderly are less likely to suffer loneliness.' It ended by calling for 'intergenerational action' to have a much larger role in tackling the challenges facing both children and the elderly in our society.

The book you hold in your hands, at the most basic level, is a prophetic call for 'intergenerational action' in our churches. We certainly don't have all the answers to your questions, but what we do have is the sense of a God-given calling to express what we believe is his heart, his desire and design for the *big family of God*, all ages and stages of life, to worship together. If generational diversity can have such a significant impact in everyday scenarios such as nurseries and care homes, how much more impact can it have when it's infused with the Spirit of God through the church at worship.

We have prayed that this book, in your hands, will not just be information but will lead to transformation—first of your own heart and mind and then of the church you belong to. In fact, over the last thirteen years or so, where we have been obedient to God in this call to write songs for, lead and speak on Worship for Everyone, one of the recurring responses we have received is that people feel we have *imparted* something to them of what God has placed on us. That is what we hope you come away from this book with—a renewed sense, born of a revelation of the truth of God and a move of the Spirit of God in your heart, of God-given vision and passion to take intergenerational action in your church. That you will build wisely the true big family of God in its local expression in your community.

A guide to the book

You can read this book any way you choose, although we have a suggested route that is the natural way the book flows. However, if you are reading this desperate for some practical help, then you can dive straight into some of the later chapters. For example, need some inspiration on how to do an all-age talk? Skip straight to Chapter 9. Or perhaps you need some tips for constructing services well—skip to Chapter 10. Still, there is a journey to the book, and you will get the most out of it if you are able to work through from start to finish. The book flows from vision and theology in Part One through to implementation and application in Part Two, concluding with appendices containing examples of talks, service structures and links to further resources.

This is not an academic book; we have tried to limit footnotes as far as possible. But in some sections, especially in Part One, it seemed appropriate and helpful to include signposting to further reading or clarification. Our main goal, though, is to keep the text in this book as simple and easy as possible to digest whilst also providing clues if you want to go deeper.

We have chosen to use the term *intergenerational worship* to be consistent throughout the book. There is a lot written elsewhere about why terminology matters and what the 'right' terminology is.[3] The main thing to know is that a church can be 'multigenerational' without being 'intergenerational'. A church that has people from different ages and stages of life within its congregation and may have multiple ministries split by age and stage (youth groups, children's groups, ministry to the elderly, twenties groups and so on) is multigenerational.[4] It only becomes *intergenerational* when those generations interact and inhabit the same space, having shared experiences and influencing one another in spiritual formation. Worship for Everyone is thus an *intergenerational* activity and goal, not merely multigenerational. It is about providing opportunity within a multigenerational community for cross-generational interaction.

The book begins with a couple of chapters exploring how your own past experience and your current vision for intergenerational worship can be interrelated. This is a key opportunity to stop and think about why you do what you do in your church. How is your intergenerational worship going? Take an audit—zoom out and think afresh. What is your vision? You will hear some of our personal story and be asked to reflect on your own.

We then guide you through some deeper thinking on a biblical foundation and framework for understanding intergenerational worship, exploring the importance of the presence of children throughout the Bible as well as broad themes like adoption and unity in the New Testament.

The journey continues by acknowledging how intergenerational worship can be difficult and identifying some of the barriers to it flourishing before framing the question more positively by asking, 'What do children *need* to thrive in church?'

Having covered some of the theory and foundational questions for intergenerational worship, in its second half the book turns to application and more practical aspects. We explore everything from choosing songs to crafting talks, constructing whole services and more. It is in the practical that your theory will be embedded and vision and values displayed.

Finally, one of the things the coronavirus pandemic has taught us, or at least amplified for us, is the interconnectedness of work, home, church and school. The boundaries have often seemed to disappear between what had previously been seen as discrete areas of family life. It is crucial for the future of the church that we grasp hold of this cultural moment and the possibilities it invites and work at ministering to all of these areas whilst understanding the core things that unite them. Our final chapters therefore focus on the areas of schools and online ministry before guiding you towards the appropriate next steps for your context.

As we turn to the opening chapter, we invite you to pray, to invite God to speak to you by his Spirit as you read this book. Whether you feel yourself an expert in intergenerational worship or a novice desperate for some help, a seasoned church pastor or a volunteer children's group leader, there is *nothing* God cannot do through your openness, availability and faith. As you approach this book, may these words echo around your heart and head and become your prayer for your community and your intergenerational worship of Father, Son and Holy Spirit.

Faith as tiny as a seed,
Faith as small as it can be
Can move a mountain.

We believe in God,
We believe in God.
We've got faith,
Faith in him.

Nothing is impossible for God,
Yes, I believe it!

Excerpt of the song 'Faith' by Nick and Becky Drake[5]

Part I

THE THEORY

1

Our story

For me, Becky, the early experience of church could have been enough to put me off Jesus for life. Growing up in a small Lincolnshire market town, I attended a traditional Anglican service each Sunday that consisted of several hymns from *The English Hymnal*, the same liturgy week in, week out and an incomprehensible sermon every time. There wasn't anything for children. There was no Sunday school, as there were very few volunteers and even fewer kids. My brothers and I made up the majority of under-sixties. The hour-long gathering was an endurance test for the three of us. We found countless ways to distract ourselves from the agitating boredom we all felt. My oldest brother would do a whole load of advanced maths on the hymn numbers set out on the old wooden hymn board and come up with some extraordinary sum. My middle brother typically fell asleep on my mum's shoulder, while I would study the patterns on the kneelers or scrape my fingernails into the wooden pews. Mum would do her best to engage us by flicking through the Bible to see how many times we could find our names—being called Rebecca, Matthew and Simon (with equally Biblical middle names), there were plenty of name-spotting points to be won!

As if this weren't a bad enough reflection of the Christian faith, even worse was the attitude of one of the church wardens. I will never forget the day I had brought my young friend to church. We were eight years old and utterly relieved as the end of the service came. As soon as we could, we darted out of the nave and arrived at the church hall first in line to get biscuits and beakers of strong orange squash—the highlight of Sunday morning. As we opened the door and reached out for custard creams, we were greeted by the church warden with a harsh 'Those biscuits are for the ladies!' Deflated and embarrassed, we sat down, biscuitless, and waited for my mum to arrive. Clearly, in this church worship wasn't for everyone but only for some (in this case, 'the ladies'!), and certainly not for children like me.

Thank goodness for my parents, who faithfully lived out a genuine relationship with God throughout my childhood. At home, there was no question I couldn't ask, prayer was part of daily life and my mum and dad modelled Jesus in how they loved us unconditionally. If only the way our little nuclear family lived and worshipped could have been reflected in the wider gathering.

Not only do I have my parents to thank, but also Spring Harvest—the second reason I count myself a Christian today. Spring Harvest, an Easter Christian conference that my family attended every year of my childhood, showed me that Christianity could be alive and relevant. It gave me Christian friends, engaging Bible teaching and songs to sing that would sustain me throughout the year. I felt thoroughly welcome there, and— even more than that—time and work had gone into planning this with every age in mind. The sessions were crafted to serve and facilitate my involvement. I learnt the joy of singing and dancing in worship; I encountered the Holy Spirit there for the first time when I was twelve years old, during sensitively led prayer ministry; I learnt to pray out loud for others over my teenage years. None of this happened through my home church—I learned it all purely during this one week of my year.

Furthermore, throughout my childhood, Spring Harvest was the one place I could be a missionary. I would happily take friends with me to the Butlin's site we met in, and many were impacted by their time spent in worship. I genuinely looked forward to this week of the year more than Christmas, and we wept on the way home each time (half grief at leaving my spiritual home behind and half exhaustion)!

Although the children's groups at Spring Harvest were dynamic and engaging for a young girl, the deepest, most lasting impact of these holidays was the time I spent together with my parents in the evening celebration. *Together* is such a key word and value when pursuing intergenerational worship. I so clearly recall the atmosphere of praise all around me. It felt uplifting and reassuring. I sensed heaven in the venue time and again over the years. I remember days we were invited forward together as a family for prayer ministry and times when I watched the whole room with their arms in the air. I also remember occasions I drifted off to sleep in my parents' arms, with a deep peace and sense of belonging. It wasn't necessarily that these sessions were crafted with children in mind, but just knowing that I was welcome and could join in with the whole body across the ages felt very special. I didn't understand everything I heard during those times in worship, but I still felt part of it, and I believe that my young heart and mind was being shaped and discipled in that space in many unseen ways.

Worshipping together without generational borders is so rich for all these reasons. It's a space where we get to learn together, unite together, feel the sense of God's family together and reflect a more complete image of the body of Christ.

One of the reasons I am so passionate today about the whole family being included in worship is that I experienced both extremes so keenly as a child. At one extreme back in Lincolnshire I may as well not have existed in the church body, and at the other end I was welcomed completely, which was hugely significant for my life. We might think today that because our children's programmes and hospitality are more kid-focussed and engaging, because we have dedicated children's pastors and rooms set aside for the youngest, we are in a different camp from the church warden I encountered as an eight-year-old girl. In some ways, of course, all of the above reflects a value placed on children that perhaps hasn't always existed in our churches. But I would also caution us to consider whether underneath the surface there are some similarities to what I experienced in my youth. Is our priority actually 'biscuits for adults' and everything that can mean in terms of our worship, or are we truly hosting a place where the newborn to the ninety-year-old are equally welcome in all aspects of church life and able to regularly worship together? Is our goal that we might encounter Jesus side by side? Or have we lost our sense of direction, and has it all become a bit of a duty? Perhaps our intergenerational worship, if we're honest, feels more like religious ritual than a spirit-filled, Jesus-centred gathering. Maybe some of us have given up on it altogether.

The fact is, it isn't easy. It is far easier to narrow our 'target market' and deliver an age-specific style of worship and teaching every week. It requires less thought, less planning, less mess, less distraction. If we make everyone in our congregation as comfortable as possible each Sunday, we'll feel it's been a success. However, John Wimber of the Vineyard Church once said, 'It's neat and tidy in the graveyard. It's alive and messy in the nursery.' I know where I would rather be!

We truly believe intergenerational worship, *Worship for Everyone*, is a vision that is worth chasing. Many have tried and have found it unsatisfactory, or too hard, and it can be tempting at this point to give up pursuing the vision. But let's not make that the end of the story! The goal isn't that we should create a monthly event that we'll have to endure, but to be part of a church community that delights in worshipping and experiencing God's presence together; that our churches might truly show a glimpse of the fullness of God's family, male and female, black and white, young and old; varied, beautiful, diverse.

We have wanted to write this book for a few years now, but a combination of hectic family life and ministry have prevented us. We've also partly delayed writing because we feel a certain trepidation! We are acutely aware that we are not giants in the world of intergenerational worship. We are essentially songwriters and parents. There are some incredible writers and theologians out there who have been studying intergenerational worship for years. But we believe that God has given us a vision that is bigger than us—and we are growing in our understanding of what it is, year by year. In some sense, we have come to see ourselves as 'commissioned' by God to both defend and promote intergenerational worship. We truly believe that God cares deeply about this issue. He cares that the church find ways to worship as a whole body—not just part. So, we believe a key element of our calling is to write songs for everyone, teach on how to do it and pursue it within our own community, as much as we can.

Worship for Everyone: how did it all begin?

If you're reading this and are somehow involved in church ministry—perhaps a worship leader or church pastor—don't let me fool you into thinking we always had a deep passion for intergenerational worship! It's highly likely you've picked up this book because something isn't 'working' in your church, or perhaps you feel stuck or lacking inspiration. Whenever we speak on this topic across the country, similar themes emerge. Do any of these statements resonate with you?

'When we have an all-age service, some people don't bother to even come!'

'The children are fine, but the adults look bored.'

'The adults are fine, but the children aren't engaged.'

'No one enjoys these services! They are a trial to be endured!'

'The action songs are cringey! The adults don't want to join in.'

'We don't know what to do about the youth—how do you engage them in all-age services?'

'We don't have any skilled all-age leaders.'

'I feel we *should* do this, but it's not bringing us much life!'

'I'm fine leading worship with adults but don't know what to do when children are in the room!'

'Do we really have to be together? Can't we just keep separate?'

'Our young parents are exhausted. They need a break from their kids!'

'We've tried and failed and have given up completely now.'

If you've nodded your head to any of these statements, then be assured you are not alone. We would have been nodding along to several of these statements back in 2003, when Nick took up his first post as worship pastor at St Paul's church in Hammersmith.

We were in our early twenties, and we had spent the previous three years in a Christian rock/pop band called Coastal Dune. (Don't worry, you're not alone if you've never heard of us—Battle of the Bands winners, 1999 Durham University!) We had enjoyed songwriting, performing across the country in a whole host of music venues, pubs, universities and underground clubs in Soho, and in between gigs, we were passionate about leading worship whenever we could. We had encountered the Holy Spirit in worship, and there was no greater joy than leading other people into God's presence, standing on the truth of what God has done in Jesus. We'd spent our teenage years at Stoneleigh, Soul Survivor and Spring Harvest, and we knew what was possible when God's people gathered together in worship. They were exciting times in the wider church and in our own lives.

So, when we arrived at this big London church, a new plant from Holy Trinity Brompton, full of people who were pursuing God and doing amazing things for him, we couldn't have felt more at home. Except that every single week there was a dedicated time of 'all-age' worship which felt to us like it jarred with the rest of what we were leading. The style was different; generally speaking it felt more dated and less varied. It often seemed like the goal was just a bit of a musical knees-up for kids! We inherited a bunch of songs that the congregation already knew, which stylistically seemed more like nursery rhymes—some set to Bible verses—and as we led the families in worship, it felt like we were being asked to be more like kids' entertainers. But then, when the children left the room, we would immediately relax and be able to create space for the Holy Spirit, through carefully selected and rehearsed songs with a variety of musical tempos, lyrical themes and grooves. All was geared at helping people to come face to face with Jesus—unlike the time of all-age worship, which didn't seem to have much of a goal, except perhaps to keep the kids happy and have fun. Not bad goals in and of themselves, but not much of an aspiration for true worship! And many of the songs felt a bit silly to adult ears or musically simple and predictable. As we looked at our congregation, the littlest at the front were fairly happy, but the entire back half of the room were not. This was not all-age.

What was our immediate solution?

We knew something didn't feel good and needed to change, but being young and lacking vision in this area, our solution was quite extreme. Nick decided to write to the PCC (the governing body) and request that the children no longer come into church! Looking back, we have often laughed at the irony of this and at how God uses the most unlikely leaders to bring change.

If you are a worship leader who dreads leading with everyone present, we have been there. If you're a church pastor who abdicates all responsibility to run the family services to someone else because you, in your heart of hearts, want nothing to do with them, then we fully sympathise!

Looking back, and this is a challenge for all leaders, we were only comfortable leading worship for a certain age group— probably around eighteen to fifty years old. Any younger or older and we weren't skilled or flexible in meeting their needs. And for some reason it hadn't dawned on us that God had called us to lead his **whole** church in worship! Without realising it, we had narrowed the calling down to a specific age group and type of person. Many of our churches have embraced a style of worship that works for one age group only and won't adapt their style or extend their skills and expertise to welcome everyone. And then we find ourselves wondering why children disengage or the youth are bored or the elderly don't want to stay. So, one question we have to ask ourselves if God has called us to lead his church in worship is: 'Am I willing to lead **worship for everyone**, or just worship for some?'

Thanks to our devoted vicar at St Paul's, Rev. Simon Downham, and the Associate Rev. Tim Stilwell, who both placed a high value on intergenerational worship, they graciously wouldn't accept that removing the children was a viable solution to the problem! So, if change was needed, *we* needed to bring the change.

We began by looking at the habit we had fallen into as a worship team. The truth was, the worship we were leading when children joined us was geared at preschoolers and everyone else suffered it. Some of the songs didn't even sing to God or about God. We sang Bible stories about characters from the Bible but didn't actually sing to God himself! So of course people weren't able to engage in any meaningful way. The songs were perfect for a toddler group or nursery-age Sunday school—but not effective or helpful for an intergenerational gathering. We will speak more about this later in the book, when we explore the key traits and attributes of Worship for Everyone songs and why getting the right songs matters so much.

So, as songwriters, the starting point for us was rethinking the songs we used for all ages. Songs, of course, are so much more than they seem. The songs we sing carry with them a set of values, a culture and a theology. Without knowing it at the start, we had stumbled into something very important; by changing our songs, we would begin to change our culture and change the whole worship experience of our church.

And that's where we began to change our style of songwriting. We began to write with the goal of uniting the church, rather than dividing it. We began writing songs that could release worship *for* everyone—both children and adults in the room. The more songs we wrote, the more God began to birth a deeper vision for what was possible.

So, as this chapter ends, we invite you to start thinking about what *your* story is. You've heard a bit of our background now, but each of you reading will have your own story to tell. What was your church experience growing up? Have you largely worshipped in age-and-stage programs, or have you experienced intergenerational (often called *family* or *all-age*) worship? If it is the latter, has it been a positive or negative experience for you? What brings you to this book? Why are you still reading it now? All of this matters!

When we gather intergenerationally, ultimately vision is everything. Without vision, the people die (Prov. 29.18), and without God's vision for all-age worship, it will surely die (or feel deadly!) in our churches. So if you've never had a vision for all ages, or you're so sick of trying that your energy has gone, that's where you need to start. It's time to get a vision!

The encouraging thing is, I'm guessing you wouldn't be reading this if your vision had truly died. The fact you've got this in your hand now is an indication of some desire for something more meaningful in your all-age gathering. In the next chapter, we're going to explore vision and guide you to create anew or re-establish your church's vision for Worship for Everyone.

Prayer for vision

Holy Spirit, please lift my eyes and fill my heart with fresh faith for what is possible in worship. I don't want myself or the church community I'm a part of to be limited by my own experiences. Speak to me and show me your desire, your heart for intergenerational worship in my church. Amen.

2
Forming a vision for all-age worship

Vision. What you see has a huge impact on what you do, how you think, the worldview you have. Think of Moses at the burning bush or Paul on the road to Damascus. Think of John on the island of Patmos. In fact, the Apostle Paul writes about the importance of 'seeing' with our spiritual eyes:

> I keep asking that the God of our Lord Jesus Christ, the glorious Father, may give you the Spirit of wisdom and revelation, so that you may know him better. I pray that the eyes of your heart may be enlightened in order that you may know the hope to which he has called you, the riches of his glorious inheritance in his holy people, and his incomparably great power for us who believe. (Eph. 1.17–19)

Paul is inviting us to be switched on to the realm of faith.[1] Not just to operate from what we can see with our physical eyes, but to lead into hope (v.18), and to lead with God's great power at work in and through us (v.19). Moreover, the Spirit is with us to give us short-range wisdom and long-range vision (v.17).[2]

We start here because it is absolutely critical to have a *faith-birthed and faith-sustained vision* for intergenerational worship in your context—a sight that can only come by tuning into God, by getting God's heart and God's perspective. Only such a vision, born of faith, will last through the challenges (and there are challenges!) of pioneering Worship for Everyone in your context. Lift your eyes to see what's *possible* when all ages worship together.

Your vision and values

So we start with a question: what is your vision for children and adults worshipping together? Do you even have one? Have you ever sat down and talked about what you're trying to achieve as a church in this area? What are your values for intergenerational worship?

Whether you know it or not, your church—like every church—has its vision and associated values on display. They are in the very fabric of what you do. You may be so deeply involved in your church that you've grown accustomed to them and you have no idea what they are any more or how a guest or newcomer may read them!

By way of example, think of your favourite coffee shop to sit in—maybe to meet a friend or to work in. If I, Nick, am on my own and I want to sit and write on my laptop, it's Café Nero every time. Why? Because I know exactly what my experience will be like if I go there. I will almost always be able to have a table and chair. The table and chair will be a good work height, as opposed to a sinking armchair and coffee table. The mood will be dark wood and blue colours, with books on some of the shelves; it will be nonintrusive in visual feel and comforting and classy in its replication of an Italian coffee house. (You're getting a real insight into me now!) Moreover, the actual coffee will be good—a large white Americano (if you were wondering) will see me through the whole writing session. This experience is reliable and consistent both chronologically (I wrote my first publication on worship there in 2013, and I'm writing this now in 2021) and geographically (the London 2013 experience was almost identical to the Birmingham 2021 one).[3]

Café Nero, in this example, is providing me with a reliable, consistent experience in their building because they have embedded their vision and values in everything they do, from décor to drinks.

Your church service is communicating your vision and values through how it looks, how people are welcomed, what kind of building it's held in, how cold or hot it is, how the children are treated, how loud, quiet, contemporary or traditional the music is and so on. So is your online content. We have to become *aware* of how we're communicating our vision and values and then become *proactive* in deliberately choosing them, rather than accidentally letting them happen.

So back to the original question. What are your church's vision and values for intergenerational worship? Have you been proactive in defining them and then implementing and embedding them to create a *culture* of Worship for Everyone within your community? Is the experience children and adults have when they worship with you *deliberately curated* based on a given vision and set of values?

Our vision

Our vision is actually very simple, and you've already seen it when you picked this book up. You've already read it numerous times. Our vision is *worship for everyone*. It's so basic, so right there in front of your nose, but so easy to neglect or miss as a goal for when children and adults are together (as we're about to see).[4]

In fact, it was so simple and yet so powerful a concept that we actually felt we needed to find a way to redefine the whole genre that we'd inherited. What do I mean by that? I mean reconsidering terms like *family worship* or *kids' worship* or even *all-age worship*. Some of these were obviously deficient—*family* excludes anyone who is not in some kind of nuclear family;

kids' worship signals that whatever is about to happen is definitely not for any adults present! We've seen this go wrong in so many churches where the leader announces 'and now a time for the kids' or the worship leader says 'we're going to do some kids' songs now', and if you're an adult in the room your heart sinks and you reach for your phone or disappear into your head and start worrying about remembering to take the bins out when you get home. Worship for Everyone puts *worship*— Jesus-centred, Spirit-dependent worship—as the main goal and the first word spoken of our vision. It also makes it abundantly clear that this worship is *for everyone*—it is aiming never to be exclusive in age or stage of life in its vision for worshipping together. This is not just family worship but worship that is also for a single thirty-four-year-old or a nineteen-year-old student or a seventy-eight-year-old grandma living on her own.

The way Becky and I deliver this vision is twofold. Firstly, we approach what we do *spiritually*. Returning to how we began this chapter, the vision must be born in and worked out through prayer and dialogue with God. Secondly, we work hard, when the opportunity arises, to lead, facilitate and create great resources for everyone to worship together well.

We do this through the following values.

Our values

We have five things that we value and intentionally aim towards for anything involving Worship for Everyone. These values apply whether to a song we're writing, a service we're planning or a five-minute slot online we're given to lead an intergenerational crowd in worship.

1 Believing in the power of unity in worship

We aim to bring down age-related barriers, particularly those between children and adults, in order to serve and build what we call the 'big family of God'. This recognition of the power of unity in worship is one of the foundational beliefs and drivers of Worship for Everyone: that God loves it when we sing and worship him as one big family of God, people who would otherwise be strangers if it weren't for Jesus in the midst of us, leading us, uniting us in and through what he has done on the cross. We believe the church displaying unity across boundaries that the world often reinforces—in this case, across age groups—is a powerful spiritual force for good. Uniting generations together in worship is such a powerful treasure for the church to display.

I have led worship 'for adults' for over twenty years, including at major conferences with thousands of adults singing together, but, hand on heart, the most powerful moments have been when I've been leading adults *and* children together in worship. I remember leading with Becky at a summer conference recently and seeing everyone from four-year-olds to forty-year-olds and beyond all singing and doing the simple actions for one of our songs, called 'Every Step'. The words go:

With me, God is with me,
Yes, he's with me every step (x2)
I know God is with me every step I go,
I know God is with me every step.

Oh, the love of God is with me every day,
Every step I take.
He will lead me on
Into his perfect plan,
Walking hand in hand.[5]

I can't express how powerful it was to see everyone in the room worshipping as one. All ages were singing together and doing simple actions with their hands to symbolise and speak of how God is with them every step, how we are one people, one family, all on a journey with God. Every one of us, no matter if single or married, young or old, shares this central dependency and need for God to be with us and to know that God is with us. This is the power of unity in the room—to see a child singing, 'Oh, the love of God is with me every day, every step I take', alongside an adult singing the same line *with the same child-like faith*.

That story reveals one final aspect of the value of unity. Worship is not something we do *to* children but something we do *with them*. We'll unpack this value and what it means practically later on in the book. What's important to note here is that we're united together because of our shared identity as 'children of God', regardless of our physical age. Worshipping together, no matter who or what age and stage is in the room, is in spiritual reality *a group of children at play in the Father's house!*

2 Using the same theology and values you have for 'adult' worship when children are present

One of the big temptations—and big mistakes—we have seen in ourselves from the early days and have witnessed at many other churches is to automatically drop your normal ('adults only!') worship values when children are present and you're suddenly faced with leading intergenerationally. By way of example, the classic move is to leave behind everything you know to be good and trusted in terms of leadership technique and worship resource in order to 'create FUN!' The thinking goes (although it's not often actually conscious thought), 'well, if there are children here, I need to become a crazy TV or YouTube presenter and the whole hour we MUST HAVE NON-STOP FUN for them!' This is especially the temptation for the 'adult' leader who never does anything with children or doesn't feel it's their natural gift. That was definitely my default when I first came to this!

But what if we just took our existing values and beliefs for worship and kept them for when children are present? We may need to *reframe* them and add to them, but if they are *right* and *true* for releasing and facilitating worship, why drop them now? It may seem like an obvious point, but it's actually very common for churches to abandon their goals and values for worship in order to generate and prioritise 'fun'. At its worst, this stems from the fear of not being able to keep everyone's interest and engagement in what is happening at the front. And our goal should never actually be to 'keep everyone happy' anyway. It'll never work. We'll come on to that later.

So, the goal of the meeting is to *worship*, and we may need to adapt our values but at the core they remain the same. For example, when I was worship pastor at St Paul's Hammersmith, the values we had developed for our sung worship were 'Adoration, Encounter, Transformation'.

Adoration—we're gathered to focus on God, to lift our hearts and voices to him, to pour out praise for who he is and what he has done in Christ.

Encounter—we believe God is real and alive and wants to meet with us today, and so we are praying for and expectant of an encounter with the risen Christ by the Holy Spirit.

Transformation—we pray for and expect people to be transformed by the working of the Holy Spirit as we worship and meet with God.

When children are present too and we are a generationally diverse gathering, these same values remain. Now, this is where we enter another topic—the understanding of children in the church. We'll look at this more later, but the point here is that *there's no junior Holy Spirit.*[6] I remember the breakthrough moment for me was when I said out loud this phrase: 'Children are just *people* Jesus wants to encounter.' For me as someone used to purely leading adults in worship, this was a breakthrough in my understanding because I knew how to lead adults into an encounter with Jesus, and so suddenly I felt empowered and able to lead children too—whereas if I had been asked to be a children's TV presenter, I would have ruled myself out straight away!

Do you see the power of keeping the same values you already have and already work within and operate out of? And do you see the importance of even writing down and articulating your values? Having clear values for your times of worship will, as in my example, release leadership and invite others to step into what you're trying to achieve in your church's intergenerational worship, even those who may have been hesitant.

One final example of how we've observed values can change when children are present in our times of worship is in the realm of songwriting for children and all ages. When we first started leading worship, the songs that were at our disposal to use did one or both of two things: teach scripture and be fun. Now, of course, neither of these goals is bad in and of itself. The point is, for us the vision of sung worship being able to facilitate intimacy and encounter with God was not reflected in any way in the songs that were available at the time for leading intergenerational worship. Our normal values for worship were not present. We'll tell you more of that story and how it drove us to begin writing songs in Chapter 7.

The theology of worship—how you understand *what it is you are doing* when you worship together—doesn't need to change either. We'll cover this in the next two chapters.

3 **Giving the same resources to children and intergenerational worship as adult ministry gets**

When we first began to teach on leading Worship for Everyone, I used to hold up two albums—an adult worship album and a kids' worship album—and ask the seminar participants to guess how much money had gone into making each one. Of course, I didn't know the exact answer, but I had a fairly good idea, having been involved in making music and recording it for most of my life. The point of the illustration was to show the huge disparity between the money that went into adult ministry compared to what went into children's ministry. Now, money isn't everything, but if you want to know what a business or an organisation truly values, see where they spend money.

It is a key value for us to ensure the same resources—time, energy and money—that are spent on adult ministry are invested in ministry to unite all ages in worship. This is really an extension of the point already made that the same worship values should be shared across generations. For example, 'excellence', based on passages such as Psalm 33.3,[7] is often cited as a key value for contemporary musical worship (and indeed has been for cathedral worship and other traditions for centuries)—why can't the same value be applied in intergenerational worship where kids are involved?

Again, by way of example, back when CDs were the thing, we would sit in the car as a family and I would take out the adult worship CD that I'd been listening to and replace it with a kids' worship CD. The difference in sounds, the mix and how the finished product came across was huge. We have since been on a mission to ensure that the songs we write and produce for Worship for Everyone are at the highest standard we can possibly achieve. Why should children have second-best quality?

Now, not everyone will be able to do that. And that's OK. Excellence is relative and about doing what you can do within your context. The point is, don't let there be a disparity between the time, energy and resources you put in for adults and for children. This can play out practically in many areas—here are a few examples from our lives, but you must work out your own way to apply this in your context:

Team—I remember the first time we planned a whole series of Worship for Everyone gatherings. It was for Spring Harvest here in the UK. When we came to plan the main themes, teaching, structure and so on, we made sure that in addition to Becky, a theologian was present (me!), a teacher was present (more experienced than us in teaching and leading children well) and a dancer was present who could help us devise actions to accompany some of the songs. We wanted to bring the very best we could to the table and we knew that that would mean working as a team on this. We'll mention the importance of teams throughout the book, but even if you're in the smallest church imaginable and you feel there is no one else to ask, we want to encourage you to pray and ask the Lord whom to bring on board with you in pioneering and developing intergenerational worship. Even if its someone from afar who can pray for you—that's team! As I often say to my kids in fun, *teamwork makes the dream work!*

Musical and production standards—Put the very best musicians and sound engineers as much on the intergenerational services as they are on the adult times of worship. When I used to run worship rotas, I remember the great temptation to assign certain musicians to the central, 'important' services. No wonder that church pastors and congregations often give up on intergenerational worship times if they've only ever experienced a drummer or piano player we would never dream of putting on team for the big adult service we've got coming up, or a preacher or speaker who would never be put on an adult service. This is how your intergenerational services can go on a downward spiral; the standard becomes such a big drop from how an adult service is run that the 'family service' becomes the one to avoid if you are a sane-thinking adult! This *must never happen*. It's all to do with agreeing beforehand that as a church you will put the same time, energy, effort, talent, prayer and money into these gatherings when children are present.

Leadership presence—Another example is the visible presence of the senior church leadership at gatherings of intergenerational worship. This is a small, easy yet hugely significant 'win' a church leader can provide. The presence of the senior leader, pastor or vicar speaks volumes as to what *they* value and what is important in the church. If the intergenerational times of worship are always run purely by you as a volunteer or by the children's pastor, then what will be communicated is that this gathering and the presence of the big family of God together are of less value and importance than other things in the church. If you're a senior leader, be present, be visible, give value. This is not just for the church pastor, but for anyone who others in the church look up to or see as being in authority—PCC members, elders, the leadership team and so on.

4 Refusing to accept that it's too hard

Our fourth and final value is to fundamentally never accept defeat or retreat from trying to facilitate Worship for Everyone, releasing the power of unity when children and adults come together to praise. This may seem an odd one. But we felt it was so important that we needed to write it down and include it. Why? Because we've seen so many churches that seem like they've given up on intergenerational worship. Either literally they don't do it any more in any way, or they limp on with what has become a ritual of a family service but not a life-giving one. It has unfortunately become worship for no one!

The temptation at that point for both the leaders of the church and those involved in making the service happen is to back down, to step back, to wash their hands of it and say, 'See, I told you, it doesn't work,' or 'This is just not our thing.' To put it bluntly, and to put it spiritually, this is precisely what the enemy wants. He doesn't want us to have good intergenerational worship culture in our churches and in our communities. Why? Because he *hates the power of unity in God's people.*

There is tremendous power in acknowledging that intergenerational worship is difficult, that there will be setbacks, knockbacks and bad times! There will be people who don't like it, children who don't get it, adults who don't attend it, but that doesn't mean God doesn't *want it.* So, it's a calling, a commitment, a vision—walk it, get it done and rise back up from setbacks to keep going. It's on God's heart and he's putting it on your heart too. He will be your source and resource. Don't give up.

Two key principles

All of this can be summed up in two very simple-to-remember and practically embedded principles for leading intergenerational worship:

1 **Elevate children**

2 **Engage adults**

If you don't remember anything more from this book, remember these two things.

What do we mean by 'elevate children'? Everything we've already mentioned to do with placing a high value on children in the church. Children are not second-class citizens (remember Becky's story about the biscuits?), nor are they spiritually 'adults-in-waiting'. They are simply *people Jesus wants to encounter*, just like the adults in the room. There is no junior Holy Spirit and there was no 'junior Jesus'! Jesus is for everyone. So, 'elevate children' means lift them up, have a high view of them, worship *with* them and not *to* them. As well as teaching them, what can we learn *from* them?

Secondly, engage adults. You would think that would be totally obvious. And it is obvious when it's just an adult gathering. But when children are present, one danger can often be an utter shift, not only in values but in focus—towards desperately wanting to engage the children. In the process the adults in the room get totally forgotten and neglected, and ultimately this can lead to them feeling undervalued themselves or embarrassed, and they start checking out from those times of intergenerational worship. This can be seen in even the simplest of things, like the eye contact from the leaders at the front. Is it focussed low down in the room—at just the children—or does the leader also look up and out and engage the adults in the room too?

In summary

You may be thinking by now, is this possible? To lead worship for everyone? To elevate children *and* engage adults in the room? To engage adults *and* elevate children?

Well, as we close this chapter out, here are two things on our side:

1 God is with us. God is for us. And intergenerational diversity and unity are on his heart. His Spirit is with us. We're not on our own attempting the impossible!

2 Other people have done it, and not only in church. J.R.R Tolkien, C.S. Lewis and J.K. Rowling, to name a literary

trinity, have all nailed it. In fact, Lewis put the challenge down brilliantly like this: **'A children's story which is enjoyed only by children is a bad children's story.'**[8] A great children's story will actually be *for everyone*. It is possible to communicate well the story of what God has done in Jesus and to lead worship in response to *that* story in a way that is *for everyone*.

Right now, the world, in its ability to unite generations, is shaming the church, which should be *the home of intergenerational unity*. Pixar mustn't have the monopoly on what should be in the very DNA of the people of God. Are you in?

Questions to consider

1 Look at your current church with a fresh pair of eyes. What values does your church currently hold for intergenerational worship?

2 What are your own personal values for worshipping together?

3 How has this chapter made you think? Has it given you any fresh perspective or offered a challenge?

4 What do you think is the biggest hurdle you currently face in moving forward intergenerationally? For example, is it resources? Buy-in from leadership? Support from the congregation? Does your community have a narrow age range? Is there a lack of skill or passion from within the church?

5 What's the one next step YOU can take to start shaping a vision or bringing change in your context?

3

A theology of Worship for Everyone: Old Testament

When you build something new, you need good foundations.

It can be tempting to rush on at this point to look at the practicalities involved in leading intergenerational worship, but for long-term success and to sustain momentum in progressing Worship for Everyone in your context, a firm grasp of a biblical framework is crucial.

In fact, one of the most powerful moments I, Nick, have had teaching on worship was when I was teaching on this specific area. It was out in Malaysia, at a fantastic institution called St Paul's Theological College, Kuala Lumpur.[1] I'd been speaking to a cohort of students the whole week on all aspects of the theology of worship, but when we finally reached the topic of a theology of intergenerational worship, the whole atmosphere changed. People were full of energy and excitement; they couldn't stop talking about what we'd discussed and learnt that morning. It was like their eyes had literally been opened to something they'd never seen or thought about. It was a really clear example to me of the Spirit working in minds and hearts to reveal the potential power of unity across generational boundaries in worship. A 'wake-up' moment that would lead to long-term commitment.

This is why it's important to spend a couple of chapters going a bit deeper before we go wider. To *move* our hearts and minds by grasping more of the biblical narrative that supports an intergenerational experience of faith. It's not possible in just two chapters to cover everything involved, and so the aim here is more to give an example of how to think and approach this topic, as well as to signpost further reading for those who want to go deeper still.[2]

The big family of God in the Old Testament

One of the passages most used to talk about the power of worship and musical praise in popular worship literature is the story of King Jehoshaphat, found in 2 Chronicles 20. The usual summary of the passage is this:

> Judah, under King Jehoshaphat, is faced with an imminent onslaught by enemy armies (the Moabites, Ammonites and Meunites). He gathers the people together to pray and fast and after a long prayer utters this memorable line: 'We do not know what to do but our eyes are on you' (v.12). Then the Spirit of the Lord comes on someone present—Jahaziel—who declares to everyone that there is no need to be afraid as 'the battle is not yours, but God's' (v.15). The next day, the king sets out for the battle but crucially places the musicians at the front of the army to sing and praise God: 'Give thanks to the Lord, for his love endures forever' (v.21). As the song is sung, 'the LORD set ambushes against the men of Ammon and Moab and Mount Seri who were invading Judah, and they were defeated' (v.22). In fact, they start fighting one another and self-destruct! The king and his army return to Jerusalem with songs on their lips and music in the air (v.27–8).

It's an amazing story and a very strong example of the power of musical worship to transform earthly situations, especially when faced with fear or what can seem impossible odds.

It's easy to miss something hugely significant.

The presence of the children.

The big prayer gathering where the king and the people sought the Lord's help was a moment *when all ages were together*. It's easy to miss it, isn't it, but v.13 says: 'All the men of Judah, with their wives and children and little ones, stood there before the LORD.' Can you imagine the melee as everyone gathered at the temple from all over Judah to prioritise seeking God together in this moment of crisis? The power of all ages standing before the Lord in v.13 at the end of the king's prayer—punctuated no doubt by babies crying to be fed and children fidgeting?

And here's the punchline—it is in *this* atmosphere, the atmosphere of the united *big family of God*, that the Holy Spirit *moves* and is at work filling Jahaziel to speak and lead the moment. All the children, all the generations, will have seen and experienced *first-hand* the dynamic interaction between heaven and earth, the Lord and the people. It's not something that happened in church to the adults and then was told to the kids when they were picked up from their groups. The children were right at the heart of the action, right in the middle of the moment. They saw the king bow down with his face to the ground in humble submission to God (v.18), they watched as their parents and other adults did the same, and then slowly they realised that they should too. With eyes to the ground, minds wondering what on earth was happening, they heard the shout of praise suddenly rise up as the Levites leaped up and praised the one true God, the God of their parents and ancestors (v.19). They saw the army go out the next morning with the worship band at the front singing praises to God, and they heard them come back later that day on their way up to the temple as harps, lyres and trumpets played (v.28). They would never forget seeing God at work. And their personal witness would become a powerful story passed on from generation to generation.

We twenty-first-century individuals tend to see the Bible as a very adult book—a book full of adults doing cool things for God. Even more so, we tend to see them as doing a lot of it solo, like superheroes. But as this example shows, look underneath the surface, do some deeper digging, and you start seeing there's a lot more going on.

When were children present?

Firstly, as in this passage, children are often present at key moments where it's easy to miss them. They may not be what the lens of the story is focussing on, but they're still in the shot. If we could just move the camera over slightly, there they all would be, coming into focus. In the Old Testament, this happens both at special assemblies or gatherings of the people of God and at the standard feast events. For example, both Moses' farewell speech (Deut. 29.10–12) and Joshua's renewal of the covenant address after the fall of Jericho (Josh. 8.34–5) have both adults *and children* present. These are not minor events but hugely significant moments. Moses, for example, addressing an all-age congregation, says: 'You are standing here in order to enter into a covenant with the LORD your God, a covenant the LORD is making with you this day and sealing with an oath' (Deut. 29.12).

By the time of Joel the prophet, this principle of gathering together for key moments as the big family of God was firmly established—'Blow the trumpet in Zion, declare a holy fast, call a sacred assembly; bring together the elders, gather the children, those nursing at the breast . . . let them say, "Spare your people, LORD"' (Joel 2.15–17). The dedication of the new wall of Jerusalem too in the time of Ezra and Nehemiah is done with a massive intergenerational celebration (Neh. 12.43).

Aside from these special events, children would also have been present at the standard feast moments of worship such as

Passover, the Feast of Weeks, the Feast of Booths and the Feast of Trumpets. Moses again, giving instructions for the Feast of Booths, makes that clear in Deuteronomy 31.12–13. Adults were also expected to be available to give answers to children present as to what was happening and why it was so important: 'When your children ask you, "What does this ceremony mean to you?", then tell them, "It is the Passover sacrifice to the LORD, who passed over the houses of the Israelites in Egypt and spared our homes when he struck down the Egyptians"' (Exod. 12.26–7).

So by being present both at planned annual worship festivals and at unplanned crisis-moment prayer meetings, celebrations and renewals, children would have frequently experienced first-hand the leading of God, the ups and downs of their people's obedience and disobedience to that leadership, the continual mercy and provision of God in the midst of awesome revelations of his holiness and might.

In summary, there were no children's groups when the Red Sea was parted.

From generation to generation

No wonder then that there was such a tradition of also passing on from generation to generation the felt, real experience of working out life with God. It is a major theme of the Psalms—e.g. Psalm 78.4: 'We will tell the next generation the praiseworthy deeds of the LORD, his power, and the wonders he has done'[3]—as well as being seen in practice throughout the Old Testament, such as with Eli and Samuel, Naomi and Ruth and, of course, Elijah and Elisha, amongst many others.

It is also seen in the great revelation of God's nature in Deuteronomy 6,[4] which is another example of 'moving the camera' over to notice something important:

Hear, O Israel: the LORD our God, the LORD is one. Love the LORD your God with all your heart and with all your soul and with all your strength. These commandments that I give you today are to be on your hearts. Impress them on your children. Talk about them when you sit at home and when you walk along the road, when you lie down and when you get up. (Deut. 6.4–7)

This major revelation of the nature of God and how the people were to respond to him in worship was given 'so that you, your children and their children after them may fear the LORD your God' (v.2). It was a truth to be embedded right in the heart of everyday intergenerational life in the family of God and there-fore to be passed on to future generations.[5]

Hannah's lantern picture

In December 2016 we were preparing to move from Oxford to Coventry to lead a church plant, and the diocese were pursuing a property purchase for us. Just a few weeks before our moving date, the plan was halted due to a problem with the survey, and we were faced with two options: either we could stay in Oxford and commute to Coventry for a short time, or we could move into rented accommodation in Coventry—a scenario we were keen to avoid, to minimise disruption to our family.

When our final Sunday at St Aldates Church arrived, the situation was still unresolved. It felt sad saying goodbye to a church family we loved, but it was also deeply unsettling not having a house to move to, or even being sure whether we were moving at all at that point! Over breakfast that morning we prayed together as a family and asked God to speak to us about our next steps. We took time to listen and share anything we felt God was saying. Hannah, who was six, had a picture in her imagination of a man carrying a lantern (she didn't know the word *lantern* but clearly described one to us). We accepted this as a word of comfort and encouragement that God would show us the way ahead, but it turned out to be much more significant.

The following day, my husband Phil and I drove to Coventry to view three rental properties. One of them—Lanthorne House—stood out as a place we could make a home, although it was just outside the city, a location that did not seem ideal for the work we were doing. Intrigued by the unusual name, I did some research and was amazed to discover that *lanthorne* is Old English for 'lantern'. Hannah's picture, combined with our good feeling about the house, seemed like confirmation that this was the house God had for us, despite our strong hesitations about renting.

Just after Christmas we moved into Lanthorne House and spent a very happy year there. Its rural location provided the rest and restoration we needed, and we discovered that there was a fantastic primary school just round the corner. During that year both our children got places at the school, which was a brilliant environment for them. We would never have chosen to begin a new ministry in temporary accommodation, but God blessed us in so many ways through our time there. He knew what we needed much better than we did, and he used Hannah's picture to confirm this step to us.

Rachel Atkinson

Identity and belonging

There was no concept in the Old Testament of personal 'individualistic' identity outside of being part of the big family of God. Everyone's life was understood as existing in interdependent relationship to others in the people of God.

We've seen an example of this already without knowing it. The person the Spirit speaks through in 2 Chronicles 20.14, Jahaziel, is given his identity and very definition *by means of his place within the wider family and tribe*: 'Then the Spirit of the LORD came on Jahaziel son of Zechariah, the son of Benaiah, the son of Jeiel, the son of Mattaniah, a Levite and descendant of Asaph, as he stood in the assembly.'

Old Testament scholar Gordon Wenham explains it like this: 'You were who you were because of the family you were born into . . . You saw yourself not as a free-floating individual, but as part of a father's house, a clan, a tribe, a people.'[6] Even the smallest of these units—the 'father's house' (*bêt ʾāb* in Hebrew)—was not merely what we would call a nuclear family but an extended family including grandparents, children, brothers and sisters and their families, and even servants and those resident from other people groups.[7] Experts think it could number somewhere between fifty and 100 people[8] and would often be a cluster of houses built around a central shared area.[9]

An example which explicitly shows us these expanding categories of interrelated identity and belonging is the notorious story in Joshua 7 of Achan, who takes some of the devoted items from Jericho that God has said not to touch. Achan is introduced like this:

But the Israelites were unfaithful in regard to the devoted things; Achan son of Karmi, the son of Zimri, the son of Zerah, of the tribe of Judah, took some of them. So the LORD's anger burned against Israel. (Joshua 7.1)

Achan's identity is found firstly in his family (Zimri), then his clan (Zerah), then his tribe (Judah).[10] Thus when he sins, it is not an individual sin as our twenty-first-century minds naturally interpret this story but a *family* sin in the most extended understanding of that word.

33

Wenham summarises this worldview helpfully like this:

Israel, the nation, was one giant firm or company in which every member had a specific place and had a particular role to play. Every Israelite saw himself or herself as a member of a firm or team, or, more precisely, a variety of teams. The most significant team was your immediate extended family, but it in turn belonged to the larger teams such as the clan and tribe. The individual's welfare depended on the success of the team to which he or she belonged.[11]

This Old Testament worldview of interrelatedness and identity as belonging to an extended family is crucial for us to comprehend as twenty-first-century people. It is not merely in this technical understanding of Israel but found throughout the arc of Scripture—Psalm 68.6 declares, for example, that 'God sets the lonely in families'. Interestingly, this interrelated understanding of identity has in recent years been brought into theological readings of the nature of the Trinity.[12] But there is no need to use the Trinity to emphasise the importance of our interrelatedness when there is such a strong foundational theological basis in the example of ancient Israel. It is also important to hold in mind as we turn to the next chapter to explore some important New Testament concepts, such as salvation as adoption.

Before we get there, there is one more move of the camera lens to be made to draw our attention to another important illustration of intergenerational action at work in the Old Testament.[13]

The leadership of a child

As usual, we'll summarise the typical reading of the heart of the story: in 2 Kings 5, Naaman is commander of the army of Aram and is a Syrian. Unfortunately he has a skin disease. Naaman goes to see Elisha the prophet, who tells him to go and wash seven times in the Jordan River to be healed. Naaman is angered by this but eventually does go ahead and is miraculously healed, declaring, 'Now I know that there is no God in all the world except in Israel' (v.15).

It's another great story from the Old Testament and displays the power of the one true God and also his heart to heal, even those outside Israel (hence Jesus' use of the story in Luke 4.27 to explain his own kingdom ministry).

But yet again, it's easy to miss something hugely significant.

The presence of a child. This time, the child is not just present in the big assembly like with King Jehoshaphat, watching, observing and participating as God is at work in the people. That would be significant, but no, here the child takes the *lead*.

Verse 2 states, 'Now bands of raiders from Aram had gone out and had taken captive a young girl from Israel, and she served Naaman's wife.' Can you imagine the absolute horror and then ongoing fear of being a young girl snatched away from her *bêt ʾāb*? Yet it is from this place of weakness and inherent vulnerability that a child speaks up and leads the adults to God— verse 3: 'She said to her mistress, "If only my master would see the prophet who is in Samaria! He would cure him of his leprosy."' This incredible display of boldness reveals a child who knows who God is and has absolute trust in God's power to heal through the prophet Elisha. As Lynn Alexander in her commentary on the passage reminds us, '[The girl] knows that God can work miracles, because she would have seen them, sung of them, and been told of them.'[14] She not only has faith in God, but she has accurate insight into *how* to access God's healing, saving power and is not afraid to share that information.

This moment of leadership from a kidnapped Israelite girl held in slavery leads to Naaman going to his master, the king of Aram, to ask if he can go and see the king of Israel and ultimately Elisha. He even tells the king of Aram directly what the girl has said. The child speaks and is heard by a king! Not only that, but Naaman's wife, Naaman himself and the king—three adults—all are led to respond by the girl's faith.

This is intergenerational action on display, and this sets us up well for a further look in the next chapter at Jesus' view of children too.

Some questions

1 What has struck you most from this chapter that you didn't know before?

2 How well do you think your church is doing at passing on 'from generation to generation' the story of God?

3 To what extent do you see your life as interdependent with others?

4

A theology of Worship for Everyone: New Testament

The big family of God in the New Testament

Having looked at some key Old Testament passages that help us understand the people of God as an extended and interrelated family, as well as the importance of the presence of children, we now turn to the New Testament.

We will aim to do two things: first, to highlight some passages that focus on the importance of children and their presence in the people of God; second, to explore a key New Testament theological concept that provides a crucial framework for understanding the importance of intergenerational worship.

Jesus and children[1]

Then people brought little children to Jesus for him to place his hands on them and pray for them. But the disciples rebuked them.

Jesus said, 'Let the little children come to me, and do not hinder them, for the kingdom of heaven belongs to such as these.'

When he had placed his hands on them, he went on from there.

(Matt. 19.13–15)

This powerful story sets up an image in our heads as readers. The disciples stop the little children getting to Jesus. Reading it for the first time, we might be thinking, what will Jesus say? What reaction will we see from Jesus? Will he affirm their decision? He has some serious 'kingdom ministry' for the adults to get on with, after all. And then comes his response: 'Let the little children come to me, and do not hinder them, for the kingdom of heaven belongs to such as these.'

Jesus loved having the children near to him.

For Jesus, their very presence represented something of the nature of the kingdom of God and the realities of God's presence. Luke knew what he was doing when he placed the story of the Pharisee and the tax collector immediately before this story in his version (Luke 18.9–14). The tax collector is the role model Jesus wants us to emulate—why? Because he is authentic, real and honest and spills out his need for God. He knows he's done wrong, and he just says it as it is. He is like a child who knows they've made a mess by scribbling with pens all over the wall (like our son Levi did recently!) and simply repentantly calls for their parent.

Jesus not only places high value on children by allowing them to be brought to him when others feel they should be held back, but also elevates them as an example of the nature of the kingdom of God. Earlier, in the previous chapter of Matthew, the disciples are wondering who is the greatest in the kingdom of God (Matt. 18.1–5). Jesus responds first without any words; instead he performs a prophetic action, a moment of drama that speaks for itself. He calls a 'little child' to his side and places the child right in the middle of the disciples:

Truly I tell you, unless you change and become like little children, you will never enter the kingdom of heaven. Therefore, whoever takes the lowly position of this child

is the greatest in the kingdom of heaven. And whoever
welcomes one such child in my name welcomes me. (v.3–5)

For Jesus, children are an example of true faith and embody
the correct posture of a life dependent on God.[2] This posture of
childlike humility is what God calls truly great, not the greatness adults often aspire to with earthly power.[3]

Jesus' elevation of children is even more radical than our
twenty-first-century minds can grasp at first read. In the first
century AD, a child would have had very little status at all. A
quarter of all children would die before their first birthday and
half before their tenth.[4] Furthermore, the wider Greco-Roman
cultural background was not something that celebrated
children or their flourishing. Rodney Stark, in his history of
the early growth of the church, writes, 'The widespread practice of abortion and infanticide resulted in a birth-rate so low
that the population was declining.'[5] Therefore, as Cynthia Long
Westfall summarises in her article 'Family in the Gospels and
Acts', 'Jesus used a child as an example of one who had status in
the kingdom because children had no status or importance—a
child was the ultimate example of humility.'[6]

Bearing in mind this low status for children, the healing of
Jairus' daughter in Mark 5.21–43 is another powerful witness
of this contrastingly high value Jesus placed on children. The
leader of the synagogue comes to Jesus, imploring his help as his
daughter is nearly dead from an illness. On his way there, Jesus
is interrupted by a woman who also needs healing. Subsequently,
news arrives (v.35) that the child has died, and Jesus should not
bother continuing his journey. This doesn't stop Jesus. He continues to the house and ends up healing the child (v.41–2) by taking her by the hand and saying, 'Little girl, I say to you, get up!'
As Anne Richards observes, '*Nothing* stops Jesus from seeking
out, coming to and healing the little girl.'[7] Not the demanding

crowds all around him, the healing on the way that took power 'out from him' (v.30), nor even the news that the girl was now seemingly beyond healing. 'Despite having very little "worth" in the human social and economic terms of that time, being a child, female and dead, yet Jesus finds in her something of complete value, worthy of saving and healing, loved by God.'[8]

Finally, in the gospel accounts we also see children as inherent worship leaders. They know where to orientate praise. In Matthew 21, when Jesus enters Jerusalem and overturns the tables in the temple (the place that is supposed to be for worship), he starts to heal people (v.14), but the adult 'worship leaders' (priests and teachers of the law) are not happy. The children present, meanwhile, are shouting at the tops of their little voices in the temple courts, 'Hosanna to the Son of David!' (v.15). Lynn Alexander comments, 'Children saw Jesus as God's Son before other people realized who He was. And they saw Him as one to be praised, and that praise was loud, spontaneous, and natural.'[9] In the face of criticism from the chief priests and teachers of the law, Jesus, of course, goes on to affirm the children's worship using Psalm 8.2 (in contrast to what he has seen in the 'adult venue'): 'Have you never read: "From the lips of children and infants you, Lord, have called forth praise"?'

It is clear that Jesus' elevation of children left its mark on those who came after him trying to follow in his way. The Christianity that emerged in the early centuries AD demonstrated a huge shift away from its surrounding culture.[10] Cynthia Long Westfall summarises this shift: 'The early church's application of the value and importance of children had an unexpected sociological and demographic impact, particularly as the church grew exponentially.'[11]

Children at play in the Father's house

As will hopefully have become clear by now, Worship for Everyone is not about 'family worship' but 'family-of-God worship'.

It is about elevating children and engaging adults together. Not just parents, but all adults. One of the theologies that lies at the bedrock of this goal and that fuels the work towards it is that of 'adoption' in the New Testament, which we will briefly explore now. Ultimately, the focus of Jesus' teaching was not on family but rather on the kingdom of God—a wider and bigger concept that includes but transcends our earthly families.[12] In the kingdom of God, we are all, no matter what our ages or stages of life, *children* of God.[13] We become *brothers and sisters*. It's a remarkable truth that has tremendous power to unite us in worship. Let's explore it now.

Adoption

There was an incredible photograph in the press recently of a five-year-old boy, called Michael, sitting in a courtroom.[14] This wasn't a trial, though; Michael wasn't being prosecuted for a crime. In fact, it was the opposite. He was being officially welcomed into a new family. He was being adopted. What made the shot particularly special was the fact that behind Michael and his new family were a large group of children and some adults— classmates and teachers from Michael's school—all waving red paper hearts they had brought along to celebrate. Like palm leaves they waved the paper hearts in the air, celebrating the arrival of a new future for Michael, the wonder of being adopted into a new family, of new identity, purpose and plans.

Adoption into a new family is an amazing thing, and as a metaphor describing a spiritual reality, it lies at the heart of the Bible's understanding of what it is to be 'saved' and to live a life in partnership with God. Romans 8.14–16 says:

For those who are led by the Spirit of God are the children of God. The Spirit you received does not make you slaves, so that you live in fear again; rather, the Spirit you received brought about your adoption to sonship. And by him we cry, "*Abba*, Father." The Spirit himself testifies with our spirit that we are God's children.

Paul here is saying something of huge importance, something that risks becoming overfamiliar but should always shock and awaken us to see ourselves and others in a new light.[15] Through the gift and reception of the Spirit of God in us, we, broken yet image-bearing humans, are officially now 'children of God'.[16] Remember, even a slave would be seen as a member of the family—so Paul could have stopped at that level in describing our place of grace in the family of God. But no, the Spirit inspires Paul to say *children* of God, fully adopted into the family.[17]

By means of the Holy Spirit

Crucially, for Paul it is the shared presence of the Spirit of God that makes our participation in the big family of God possible. The Spirit does three things here: first, the Spirit *leads* us in this life and in relationship with one another and God; second, the Spirit *activates* ('brought about your adoption') our new identity of belonging to a new kingdom family; third, the Spirit confirms to us that this *is true* ('testifies'). He embeds this new reality in our inner and interrelated lives.

How incredible that God would choose to describe the impact of his presence, power, purpose and plans in human life as *like being part of a new family*—an eternal, loving reality. As the Reformer John Calvin wrote: 'he could not attest his own boundless love toward us with any surer proof than the fact that we are called "children of God"'.[18]

Over the years we have tried to express this central truth in some of the songs we write. Two of them in particular carry this message that lies at the heart of intergenerational worship—Worship for Everyone. Here's the second verse and chorus of one of our very first simple action songs, 'Big Family of God':

Some of us have curly hair,
Some of us have specs to wear,
All of us have different families,
Some of us are very loud,
Some of us don't make a sound,
That's because we're different, you and me.

But God loves everyone he's made,
God loves each of us in a special way.
That's you, and you, and you and you,
You and you, and you and you,
God loves you; God loves you.
That's you, and you, and you and you,
You and you, and you and you,
We're part of the big family of God.[19]

This song expresses this central truth that all of us are very different to one another and yet utterly loved by God; that we may come different from earthly families, but we are now welcomed in, anchored within and celebrated as being part of God's big (adopted) family.

A more recent song called 'God Is Good' articulates the theology through its verses like this:

Here we are, people of faith,
Some with smiles, others with fears that they face.
Here we come, ready to bring who we are.

Here we are, children of God,
Family, joining together as one.
Here we come, ready to sing who you are.[20]

There is nothing wider, richer, deeper nor more substantial than this truth that we are loved by God and invited to take our unique place in his family. This is a foundational belief of Worship for Everyone.

Through Christ

This adoption into the family of God happens by means of the Spirit, as we have seen, but also crucially through what Christ has won on the cross. The writer to the Ephesians in Chapter 2, verse 18 says this: 'For through him (Christ Jesus) we have access to the Father by one Spirit.' The author of Hebrews puts it poetically when he writes: 'Both the one who makes people holy and those who are made holy are of the same family. So Jesus is not ashamed to call them brothers and sisters' (Heb. 2.11). We are brothers and sisters of Jesus himself—he's part of the family by very nature of his divinity, we purely by grace. Quoting from Psalm 22.22, Hebrews puts in the mouth of the risen Jesus the following: 'I will declare your name to my brothers and sisters; in the assembly I will sing your praises' (Heb. 2.12). The following verse (v.13) goes on to do the same with Isaiah 8.13: 'Here am I, and the children God has given me.' It is no coincidence that, as we saw earlier, Jesus in his earthly ministry called for the children to literally come close to him and be allowed to stand alongside him (Matt. 19.14). What a beautiful image of the big family of God, the kingdom family, gathering together around the risen Jesus as he leads us, his brothers and sisters, in praise of the Father.

A new family

The word for 'family' in the Greek text only occurs once in the letters of the New Testament, and it's in Ephesians 3.14–15: 'For this reason I kneel before the Father, from whom every family (*patria*) in heaven and on earth derives its name.' It is fascinating that the only time this word is used is in the context of a prayer for the *wider new family of God*. Paul is making a link firstly between the nature of God as a parent ('Father') and the derived nature of earthly families (*patria* from the Greek *pater* for 'father'). Subsequently, he then extends this logic to the filling of the Father's likeness and character into the new big family of God:

> I pray that out of his glorious riches he may strengthen you with power through his Spirit in your inner being, so that Christ may dwell in your hearts through faith. And I pray that you, being rooted and established in love, may have power, together with all the Lord's holy people, to grasp how wide and long and high and deep is the love of Christ, and to know this love that surpasses knowledge—*that you may be filled to the measure of all the fullness of God*. (Eph. 3.16–19)

This entire passage in Ephesians emerges from a wider focus in the epistle on community, unity and the metaphor of the body for how the new family of God works together.[21] The new family we all now belong to, whatever our earthly family, is the 'Lord's holy people' (v.18) or what Galatians 6.10 calls the 'household of faith' or 'family of believers'.

In summary, this theology of salvation as adoption and the associated familial terms used to describe the spiritual reality of believers now living in Christ by the Spirit represents a deepening and widening of what it originally meant to be part of the 'father's house' for ancient Israelites. Whatever earthly family we have, we now belong to a bigger, wider, deeper, everlasting family. This fact unites us in an incredibly powerful way regardless of our earthly ages and stages of life.

An image of kingdom family

Intergenerational worship is so important because in its broken, non-perfect, messy way, it displays here on earth a spiritual reality that lies right at the heart of God's interaction with us. Worship that has every age and stage of life represented acts as a signpost and symbolic statement as to *what God is actually about*. It displays not only his heart but his intent, his salvation plan, his grace, his long-term (eschatological) purposes. God desires no one to miss out on being a part of his family and he has made a way for anyone to join through adoption in Christ and participation by means of the Spirit ('we were *all* given the one Spirit to drink', 1 Cor. 12.13).

There are many dimensions to this display of the big family of God in worship, but one of them has to be celebration. Just as those classmates and teachers celebrated the adoption of five-year-old Michael by waving their homemade hearts in the courtroom, so we, when we gather together, celebrate what God has done. Not only has he done it for each and every one of us (saved us into his family) but he is doing it afresh for anyone new in our midst that day, for anyone visiting, looking in to what we do; he is beckoning, calling and inviting them by his Spirit to join in this new family.

Our gatherings *have* to look, sound and feel like the kind of family you'd want to be in. To put it plainly, your church's intergenerational gatherings are a key way your church can communicate salvation. The big story of God is displayed in the big family of God *enjoying* God together here on earth. We worship together because, in doing so, we display God's own heart for his creation to be restored to right relationship with him through Christ, by the Spirit. We worship together to display God's design for all of us to become children of God, brothers and sisters of Christ. Children at play in the Father's house. Intergenerational worship is *kingdom family* on display.

Christ-centred, spirit-dependent worship

As we come to close this chapter, there are two further corollaries from what we have explored that are crucial for forming a foundational theology of intergenerational worship: the centrality of the Spirit, and the centrality of the risen Christ to our gathered worship. As we have already seen in Chapter 2, one of the keys for building intergenerational worship in church is not dropping all the previously established values for adult worship when children are suddenly present. This is a great temptation but a great mistake.

One way this plays out is with theological values—for example, and in particular, our understanding of *how worship 'works'*, i.e. our theological framework for gathered worship that helps us lead it, prepare for it and pray for it well. In this instance, if our gathered worship is to be both authentically and identifiably Christian (i.e. Trinitarian) as well as powerful and 'real' in its participation in God's Trinitarian life, then it must be both Christ-centred and Spirit-dependent.[22] Holding this theology not only for adult worship but for intergenerational worship is vital. It ensures that our emphasis doesn't swing too far towards relying on our own abilities to 'make worship happen', to 'be fun' and at worst 'to entertain'. It may well be that a value placed on fun in intergenerational worship is important in the mix, but it must be held within the deeper, consistent theological values that have been established already for *all* worship. What this means in practice is that there will be *prayer* for the Spirit to lead and to be at work in intergenerational worship times; there will be a proactive desire to ensure worship is Christ-centred and rich with the story of the cross, even if it's less traditional or liturgical in its framework or non-eucharistic in its form.

Unity

Over the course of these two chapters we have tried to highlight some of the biblical theology that we think is helpful for anyone wanting to explore and grow in pioneering greater intergenerational worship in their context. This has included a major focus on elevating the importance and value of children in worship through exploring some Old Testament and New Testament passages. However, the overall arc has been one of discovering what it means to be part of the family of God, from Old Testament beginnings through to New Testament redefining and widening of the concept. We have seen how there is a place for everyone in the big family of God through what Christ has done on the cross and the power of the Holy Spirit to transform. We are now all sons and daughters of God by grace, reborn to dance and sing in the Father's house as children gathered around our heavenly brother, the risen Jesus. In this place of play, there can be amazing unity. Unity across all that divides us—including generational barriers. We, as the church, need to be a place that leads the way in displaying this kind of unity for the world to see. For where there is unity, there is God's blessing:

> How good and pleasant it is when God's people live
>   together in unity!
> It is like precious oil poured on the head, running down
>   on the beard,

Running down on Aaron's beard, down on the collar
of his robe.
It is as if the dew of Hermon were falling on
Mount Zion.
For there the LORD *bestows his blessing, even life*
forevermore. (Ps. 133)

Questions to consider

1 What has struck you most about this chapter? Has anything taken you by surprise?

2 Are there deeper ways that you think your church needs to welcome the little children in, as Jesus did? Or do you feel content with how children are elevated in your setting?

3 How could your church move from 'family worship' to 'family-of-God' worship, so that all feel included?

4 How could this theological framework help to change the mindset and culture of your congregation?

5

What makes all-age worship so difficult?

Maybe by now you're starting to feel filled with vision or excited about the possibilities of intergenerational worship. Maybe, as happened to us, a lightbulb is beginning to go on. But you may also be realising that this is going to need some culture change, and before change can be implemented it's important to examine some of the hurdles that might be standing in the way. In this chapter, we're going to reflect on some of the challenges you might be facing that need overcoming.

Audience, audience, audience!

There are many reasons why intergenerational ministry is hard. Whenever we speak to churches and leaders about Worship for Everyone, we ask the room for a show of hands to find out who enjoys leading all ages and who dislikes it or struggles to like it. We ask them whether they find it easy or difficult. Almost always, the majority struggle and find it hard. Over time, this has led many churches to minimise their intergenerational gatherings to either very short interactions or very infrequent ones. Some have given up altogether and have settled for age-and-stage ministry the whole year round.[1] Many have even been met with serious opposition—church members walking out because 'it's not their kind of thing' or complaints from others who want 'their normal service back'. It's very hard to lead if there isn't buy-in and support from the church family, and it only needs one or two to be resistant and critical to deeply affect your ability to persevere through change.

When we lived in London I, Becky, spent several years working in press and public relations. One of the first and most memorable things my boss said to me when I was learning the ropes was 'this job is all about audience, audience, audience'. The repetition of this word stood out! She went on to advise that even when I think I know my audience, I need to narrow it down further. It wasn't enough to say that my message was for women. She would ask me, 'Young women? Retired women? Which postcode specifically? Are they generally single or married? What interests do they have? What do they read?' The questions went on. I soon learnt that sending a very general message or advert to a broad group would generate very little engagement; however, the narrower my target market, the more I could specifically tailor my message and use the right media to engage and impact their behaviour.

So it's no surprise that when we come to such a broad 'target market' as 'all ages', it can indeed be very hard to engage everyone! If, coupled with that, there is a lack of resource or vision, the whole thing can begin to feel stale and tokenistic. Once something is a token nod 'to the kids' it becomes boring and tiring. It fails in reaching one of our two key goals: engaging adults (it likely doesn't truly captivate children either!).

Community and humility

It is important nonetheless to remember that unlike a PR campaign, our times together in worship are not just selling a message or product but are times of community, times to worship and encounter God's presence and times of serving one another with humility as the big family of God. Our starting point must again come back to the core values and a recognition that, in and of itself, it is good to be together. It is important and powerful to unite across generations no matter what we may personally feel as individuals. We may not like every element of the service, nor does it have to be perfectly pitched to any one of us—there's a bigger story going on! As we saw in the previous chapter, being *together* is an important reflection of God's image and an important part of our discipleship, even if sometimes there are components of the service that we don't love.

If you're a leader, being honest and direct about this with your church may help switch on that lightbulb—explaining that it's hard to get this right, but more than anything you want your community to unite and throw themselves into being together. Again, if you can bring some vision to this, it will help people to be more tolerant of the noise or the different style or whatever it is that they struggle with. The hope is that in time they will begin to see and experience the beauty of being a whole family together, even if the style isn't always their top preference.

It's therefore important as part of auditing where you are as a church to think through and acknowledge some of the challenges—perhaps historical ones, perhaps ones present right now in the community. Here are some of the main areas of difficulty we have encountered in working with churches, to help you think through what is going on in your own context.

Challenges

1 **People resources**
   Many of our churches are filled with generous and devoted volunteers who long to see God's kingdom come both in and out of the church walls but don't always have the skills or experience needed to lead intergenerational worship. Some churches may have a children or youth pastor who can lead the way, but others won't have the necessary

communication or leadership skills to draw everyone together. The same goes for the lead pastor or vicar; some will feel confident in leading all ages in worship, and others will simply feel they lack the skill or experience to address children as well as adults.

2 **Ministry ideas and resources**
Churches often find it hard to lead intergenerationally because they haven't found good resources or don't have the time and skill to create their own. Finding the right songs (as outlined in Chapter 7) and selecting good themes that can work well across generations is key to building a successful intergenerational culture and getting buy-in from the congregation. We have sat through services where all the intentions were good, but a combination of dated songs and uninspiring spoken material meant that no one really was engaging much in the worship or being challenged in their faith. Finding the balance of accessibility and depth in resources and delivery can be a hard thing to get right.

3 **Financial resources**
Intergenerational ministry, like any other ministry, needs financial resource. This can range from buying materials to facilitate a response to the talk or sweets to be handed around in the offering through to the expense of building a backdrop for a big service such as Christmas or Easter. It can also be the ability 'behind the scenes' to send people on training courses or to conferences—whatever it takes, like any other ministry, to build and invest in a culture of intergenerational church life. Of course, it's absolutely possible to worship with no financial resource at all, but having a budget for intergenerational ministry and worship can really help with thinking and planning creatively. It's

amazing how many churches give up on all-age services or ministry but have never invested in them financially the same way they have in other areas.

4 **Getting stuck in a rut**
Thinking intergenerationally shouldn't be just a tag-on or an extra to the normal service. This is where things begin to feel tokenistic. Many churches struggle because they try to slot in a 'kids' moment', often out of a sense of duty. Our observation is that children often find this embarrassing—they don't want to suddenly be stared at and expected to respond! They are far more comfortable often observing and then engaging at their own pace. Equally, the huge danger is that adults tend to switch off at this point, as it seems what they've been asked to attend is a children's performance of some kind.

5 **Fear**
Fear can play a big part in limiting our leadership across all areas of ministry. Moving forward into a greater level of intergenerational engagement will demand courage from those responsible. We will need to accept that some people won't like it because we're asking the members of our congregations to step into a deeper level of commitment to each other. As discussed in earlier chapters, the way our culture has moved away from an interconnected understanding of life with one another and God means many can find this uncomfortable. This may lead to fear that some will walk out, as we've already mentioned. It may lead to fear that financial giving will go down. It might trigger fear of failure or fear of rejection. But God does not want us to be bound by fear. In fact, we won't easily move forward with a fresh vision if we allow fear to rule our decision making. We may need to bring our worries at this point before God, whose

perfect love promises to free us from the fears that so easily hold us back. If God's heart is for a united church, we needn't be afraid. Again, we know this to be true for so many areas of leading in church life, and yet somehow we often don't wish to take the risk when it comes to pioneering something of intergenerational ministry. Trust God, be bold, be strong!

Which of these areas is the principal challenge for your context? You may want to reflect on these personally or with others in your church as part of the vision and values casting. Either way, acknowledging the problem is the first step towards building an exciting new future—which is what we're going to help you with, starting with the next chapter.

Questions to reflect on

1 What makes all-age worship hard in your context? Is it a lack of resources, support, experience or something else?

2 Do you identify any fears within yourself as you think about implementing a new vision for all-age worship?

3 What's the one next step that would help to address the challenges? Do you as the leader need to champion intergenerational worship in your context? Perhaps you need to invite that naturally gifted communicator in the congregation to be on team? Do you need to invest in getting your worship team or musicians on board with the vision? Or perhaps a shift in budget and finance is the starting place for you.

'Jesus looked at them intently and said, "Humanly speaking, it is impossible. But with God everything is possible."' *(Matt. 19.26, NLT)*

6

What do children need?

One of the most helpful things for us as adult worship leaders when we were learning to lead with children present was to think through and learn about what children *need* in order to be comfortable and therefore able to engage and participate in our times of all-age worshipping together.

When our own children were very little, despite the best intentions of our church at the time, big church gatherings were sadly not a place they felt very happy at first. They've all grown up in busy, large churches, and the combination of noise, echo, loud music and lots of people was often an overwhelming mix for our highly sensitive children. We used to look with curiosity at the children who seemed to bounce happily into church, oblivious to the immense social and auditory stimulus around them! As our four children have grown older, they've learnt to manage and adapt to our church culture and environment remarkably well, but when they were little it was at times too much for them to cope with.

What this personal story illustrates is that children are as different in their temperaments and personalities as the rest of us. A note of caution therefore is important in attempting here to summarise what they 'need'. The extraverts will have different needs from the introverts. The highly sensitive children will have different needs from others. However, there are some broad categories that do unite children and provide some helpful clues for what they require to thrive in worship together. We're focussing here on children; however, what we might discover as we explore the following points is that many of the things children need, adults across the generations need too.

1 **Belonging**

We all need to belong. From the family we are born into to the school friends we make to the colleagues we later work with and the church community we are part of, belonging is central to our sense of identity, confidence and happiness.[1] Historically, churches have at times got this very wrong when it comes to children. The example from Chapter 1 of being admonished for picking up a biscuit is the opposite of being treated with belonging. In fact, in that moment, I, Becky, didn't belong at all. The biscuits were for 'the ladies'. They were 'in' and I was 'out'. Does it remind you of the disciples stopping the children from 'belonging' by getting close to Jesus in Luke 18?

While most churches have come a long way and would un-doubtedly be appalled by this kind of attitude today, there can still be some subtle messages we give our children that can communicate they don't belong. Does your church go to town on snacks and refreshments for the grown-ups but just do breadsticks for the kids? Are your adults allowed to stay in the main building throughout the service while any children are sent out every single time, some against their will? Are noisy babies tutted at, so that young, tired mums feel obliged to retreat to a foyer and sit on their own without any further contact?[2] Sometimes parents appreciate having a space outside the meeting they can retreat to if their little ones are noisy, but one thing we've done in our current church is ensured there's an audio feed into the foyer from the main service as well as nice sofas and coffee, so no one has to miss out and community can form.

Children need to feel that, as they walk into church, they couldn't be more loved and appreciated; they couldn't be more welcome; their noise doesn't offend. Even the simplest things can make a huge difference. For example, when they are in church, they need to be spoken to. They need to be spoken to on the door, as part of the church's welcome. Other adults need to acknowledge and speak to them rather than focussing on their parents, which can make the children seem invisible or unimportant. They also need to be spoken to when they remain in the main gathering. It's not actually that hard to adjust your framing of content slightly to address the room in a way that's accessible for all ages. As we'll see in Chapter 9, this is not a dissimilar approach to ensuring your gatherings are accessible to new Christians or nonbelievers, so is a good practice anyway.

If your church is already committed and engaged in age-and-stage ministry, so that the children leave the main service (or perhaps don't come in at all), it is crucial that their presence in the family of God isn't totally ignored. Perhaps you could have the children in church to pray for them before they leave for their groups. Perhaps older children or youth could share what they have learnt before they go home. If your church prays for people at the end of the service, perhaps they could return for that and be encouraged to take part in praying for others. In our current church, Gas Street in Birmingham, we've had some very special times when children, supported by parents or older adults, have laid hands on the sick and prayed or have been encouraged to ask God for a word or picture for another congregation member. The faith of our little ones is so often wide and high, and their simple prayers can reap incredible fruit. All of this aids a sense of belonging. It communicates to our children that they are valued and their spiritual life is of interest to the whole church.

2 **Familiarity**

Children gain confidence from knowing what to expect. For some this is absolutely essential—many children with additional needs or more anxious temperaments will struggle with change or surprises. Therefore, having a routine for our children at church will build confidence and will also aid that sense of belonging. For this reason, when we were at St Paul's we had a time of gathered intergenerational worship every single week. Children knew as they entered the building that they would sing and pray with their families for twenty minutes at the start of every service. We worked hard to make the sung worship familiar whilst not getting stuck in a rut. We led a wide range of songs but would carefully introduce new ones, teaching them clearly and then repeating them in future weeks so that they, too, became familiar. Children want to be able to sing along to something they know! For those who can't read, it's even more important that part of their time in worship is familiar.

We've observed over the years that where churches have opted for purely an age-and-stage programme and don't bring the children into an intergenerational gathering on a regular enough basis, they find that when they do, things are much harder. Children who are not familiar with the adult room surroundings will often find it really hard to engage and express that either by letting out energy or conversely by switching off and becoming very passive (usually ending up on a device). Others feel daunted by the bigger space, and the lack of familiarity can feel overwhelming. There are too many new things to process!

We want our gathered church experience to feel safe and be part of a child's routine—otherwise, what happens when they grow older and have never participated in a time of collective sung worship or listened to a talk before? Discipling our children into a familiar environment sets them up to feel it's an essential part of their future life. But we need to be careful to ensure the aim isn't to conform our children to 'our' space but rather to create times of shared space where we mutually relate, learn and worship together in a meaningful way.

3 Acceptance

Who doesn't need to be accepted? So much of school life is about performance and ability and following the rules. In contrast, church needs to be a place where God's unconditional love is shown and 'rules' for children are only present if they really have to be! If children constantly feel they need to sit up straight and be quiet they will, in time, not want to return. Children need permission to be children. Yes, they need to respect one another and respect adults present, so random shouting and screaming in worship or prayers is not going to be a great idea, but a bit of noise and chatter is normal. Babies cry, toddlers get very upset over small things, teenagers may not want to participate and would rather sit down at times or text. What churches often fail to realise is this is a long game. Don't judge a child's reaction in the moment as the be all and end all of their spiritual formation.

The aim is for children to grow up feeling church is a place for them. It is *their* place as much as adults in the past felt it was theirs when they reserved pews or seats. If we allow children and young people to simply *be in the space* with us without overloading them with our 'rules for engagement', then over the long term they will have a positive view and memory of gathered church. This, of course, is a baseline aim. The higher goal is that they grow and mature in their relationship with God, through attending church. But at the least, a good foundational principle is that we want our children to feel accepted in the worship space and within the church community. Unfortunately many churches have historically not even managed to do this.

As parents, we can play a big role here. Dare to allow your children to take the lead in their approach to church. If they want to stay with you and miss their age-and-stage group sometimes, let them, and see if they get something different from being alongside you. At different stages in our children's lives we have done this. In fact, in twelve years of parenting we've barely sat in church alone without at least one child. Our second-oldest child has been particularly impacted by having permission to take a break from his church group. He has enjoyed watching the worship happening around him, and over several months recently (pre-COVID) we witnessed a growing engagement in him. He went from observing to joining in the singing. He began to listen to the talks and ask us questions about them after church. We became truly delighted to have him with us, rather than viewing his presence as a nuisance or a distraction from 'our' time of worship, which we may have been tempted to think at one stage. It's been a really important shift for us as parents.

So, if children want to sit down and observe the rest of the congregation instead of standing to sing, let them—they might be absorbing what God is doing in the room and in others as they watch the faces of those around them. If they are little and want to run around and dance, let them! They might be inspiring others older than them to become a little more undignified in their praise! And if they don't understand everything, encourage them to ask questions about God without any judgment. As parents, we have been asked everything under the sun and many boundaries have been pushed. Even when inside we might be thinking in mild panic, 'Argh! Have I discipled this child properly?', we try our best to be unshockable and give them full permission to think and say what's going on in their curious minds. Knowing they are loved and accepted is foundational.

4 Purpose

Rachel Turner's book *Parenting Children for a Life of Purpose* is an excellent resource for families wanting to explore purpose for their children more fully.[3] We all need to have a sense of purpose. This is a critical area that we can participate in within our churches and intergenerational ministry. No one thrives if they feel their contribution isn't worth anything. We also don't want to raise a generation of spectators who judge church mostly on how it meets their needs or makes them feel. As we've seen in the previous chapters, church is as much about what we can bring and give to the big family of God.

Most adults reading this will know that when you serve at church, you feel more connected. If you're a worship leader, musician or singer, you'll feel a real sense of reward when you've seen others engage in worship; those serving refreshments will be boosted by the smiles and appreciation of thirsty or tired church members as they pick up their much-needed morning coffee. Those involved in welcome will feel a sense of purpose when a new person enters the church and they have the privilege of putting them at ease at this important moment as they walk in.

Again, it's not revolutionary, though often overlooked, to state that children need the same sense of purpose! They can welcome, they can start getting trained up alongside musicians or be involved in choirs, they can write and read prayers, they can help serve drinks, they can tidy up toys, they can look out for a new child at church and make them feel included. At Gas Street, one of our joys has been seeing a twelve-year-old member of our church step up to play the drums in the worship band. He began by sitting alongside one of our older drummers, watching. He then took on one song that he had rehearsed well. And now, as a teenager, he plays regularly as part of our worship team. Church leaders and parents all have parts to play in ensuring their children are aware of their purpose at church. This is a great shift away from consumerist culture. We need to start urging our children to see church as a place they can give and serve God. And our churches need to find opportunities to encourage people of all ages to play their parts.

5 **Fun**

This is a tricky one—and it's no accident that it's the final point in this list! Many churches make the mistake of starting with it. We think children, we think fun. Aiming for fun above all else can act to displace all your pre-existing values for worship, as we've discussed in previous chapters. Another problem is that fun is so subjective. As parents of four children, we know that loud music and dancing might be fun for our daughter but horrendous for one of her younger brothers. For him, reading quietly for an hour is blissful, but for his big sister that's just like being at school and it's the last thing she wants! We've got one boy who is incredibly sporty and would love to play football at the back of church, but another son who is not a football fan and would be terrified if he had to join in with a children's church football game.

So, having a goal of 'fun' is not as straightforward as it sounds; however, it's listed here because church *cannot be dull and uninspiring*! This applies across the generations, but as adults we do have a higher tolerance for a bit of boredom. The sermon can be a bit off one week or the music a bit out of tune and it's unlikely we will leave the church. But for our children, if their experience of coming to church is repeatedly not fun at all, they will in time switch off, especially as the culture around them Monday to Friday is providing constant fast-paced, new and exciting content online. Our experience of church, whoever we are and whatever age we are, can often be logged in our hearts, minds and memories as our experience of *God*. God is never dull and uninspiring!

In our Worship for Everyone gathered services, joy is a key value. We prefer the language of joy, as it's deeper and richer than 'fun', whilst as a term it also acknowledges the Spirit as the source for the joy in the room, as joy is a fruit of the Spirit. There are ways to unite around joy that are less likely to alienate. An opening quiz done well for the whole range of ages in the room is often a sure, simple way to release joy for everyone—or even handing out some surprise sweets with the collection bag one week! More crucially for sustaining long-term culture, leading services in a tone and manner that encourages everyone present will cultivate joy (and therefore give permission to have fun).

What is crucial in this is we mustn't put ourselves under too much pressure to be constantly *entertaining*. The Spirit of God moves through so many aspects of our gatherings that aren't outwardly fun, and like me at Spring Harvest, if a child feels accepted and loved in the room they're in, they can be content and have deeply meaningful spiritual formation without being wildly entertained.

These five areas are a glimpse at what children need when we gather to worship. They are mainly learnt from our own experience, so there is a lot more for you to explore in this area if it's new to you, but we hope they help you to think more deeply about your own context. In a moment there are some questions to help you reflect, but in ending this chapter there is one headline truth to leave you with.

In his research for his book *Children in Worship*, Lance Armstrong (not the cyclist!) found that, beyond immediate family, the most significant factor in children growing into having a faith of their own was the influence of a significant other individual or group of people in Christian community with that child (in the local church, at Christian camps, attending events and so on).[4] Ivy Beckwith in her book on children's ministry agrees, arguing that being *in the midst* of other people's faith stories in an intergenerational setting will have more of an impact on a child's memory than any number of Bible stories or facts they may be taught in an age-specific group.[5] This research, along with the theology we have explored in Chapters 3 and 4, all point to the simple truth that intergenerational action is critical for children's spiritual formation. That's what children need—no matter precisely how you work it out in your context.

Questions to consider

1 How is your church community doing in creating a welcoming space for children?

2 Are there opportunities in your gatherings for children to serve and have a sense of purpose?

3 How are you doing on the fun/joy scale?

4 What one step could you take to better meet the needs of your children?

Part 2

THE PRACTICE

7

Using songs in all-age worship

How much joy we can bring
To our King if we let ourselves sing

Bring your praise
Give him your heart
Young and old
All together now

Everybody sing! Everybody sing! (x2)

Excerpt from 'The Singing Song' by Nick & Becky Drake[1]

Songwriting and song selection

Songs are culture carriers. Their musical style, their lyrical content and the way they are led can communicate so many of your values as a church. Songs are therefore linked to your vision. Once you've established what you're aiming for in your gatherings and your theology of intergenerational worship, the value of choosing songs and resources carefully will become clear. It will immediately eliminate certain pieces from your intergenerational song list—or it might inspire you to begin such a list for the first time! Maybe, like us, you will find yourselves having to write your own songs.

We see the songs we use as tools to enable *everyone* in the room to encounter Jesus. As we've looked at in previous chapters, our values for worship don't change according to whether children are present or not. Children are people Jesus wants to encounter, just like adults. So, the songs we use and how we use them all share the aim of leading people to worship Jesus and experience the life of God by the power of the Holy Spirit. Of course, we take into account other values and principles as to what children find helpful, as mentioned in the previous chapter, but the core values remain the same.

Although those core values don't change, the things that make it easier for children to engage and participate in worship *do* have an influence on the songs we use and the songs we write. When it comes to times of intergenerational worship, we may need to re-examine the type of songs we choose. Those we select when only adults are present may or may not work when children join us (often lyrical complexity or musical style is the limiting factor).

Conversely, as we discovered early on our journey as worship leaders, the songs we used at that time in all-age services *only* engaged the preschoolers. That's where our own songwriting began. We wanted to plug a gap and try to write songs with lyrics that would be accessible but still meaningful for all. Lyrics that would not describe God but encourage a response to God— that would not just teach God but release worship of God. We wanted musical interest too, so that the songs would be things musicians would *want* to play. After all, if the church musicians or worship team aren't into the songs we sing at church, how can we expect the congregation to want to sing them or be led into joining in?

We now talk about these as Worship for Everyone songs. The name Worship for Everyone originally came about because we felt that 'all-age' had become stigmatised in many churches and was associated purely with kids—and sometimes with failure. 'Family worship songs' similarly had become associated just with families, and the very nature of the title excludes anyone single or not with their family. The final title 'kids' songs' is obviously not intergenerational in any way! We wanted a new phrase to capture exactly what we were aiming for—songs that released times of worship that truly were for everyone and not just for some. Of course, this doesn't mean that no other songs will work, and indeed we use other songs when we lead, but we do believe that there are certain key principles to our songwriting that are helpful to tease out for any context and for choosing your own resources for intergenerational worship.

Song elements

One of our favourite places to teach over the years has been the Worship Central Academy, which began at Holy Trinity Brompton and is now run from our church Gas Street in Birmingham. Because these students are the next generation of worship leaders, it always feels exciting and like a privilege sharing our vision with them. Invariably lightbulbs go on for them as we unpack what we believe is God's heart! One of the main purposes of those sessions has been to help them identify which worship songs will be most effective at helping the whole church to connect with God. We have encouraged them over the years to examine songs according to the following categories, which may also be helpful for you as you think about which songs to hold on to and which to let go of when all ages are present.

1 **Theme**

Think carefully about the theme and lyrics of the songs. Try to include songs that everyone can unite around. One of our early songs, 'Big Family of God', mentioned in previous chapters, has been used extensively over the years because it does the very thing it's singing about. It unites! It's a song that's for everyone, a song that not only sings about God's love but declares God's love over each person present. No one is excluded. The chorus 'that's you and you and you and you and you and you and you and you! God loves you! God loves you!' invites the whole church to point at one another while declaring this truth to each person in the room.

There will be some topics in our worship that are particularly helpful for all ages. If you have spent time with children, you'll know that they are often in awe of creation, for example. They love animals, find the autumn leaves exciting as they crunch through them and gaze in wonder as snow falls. Singing about God and creation is likely to engage a child, and grown-ups are not dissimilar, appreciating sunsets, mountains and newborn babies. Our song 'Creator God' picks up on this theme and has also become much sung across British churches and schools.

Creator God
You put the stars in outer space
You popped the freckles on my face
And all the fish that swim and all the birds that fly
Are part of your incredible imagination

Creator God, we're singing to the
Creator God of all the world
Creator God, we celebrate you, we celebrate you!

You spread the ripples through the sea
You painted stripes on every bee
And all the grass that grows and all the leaves that fall
Are part of your amazing plans for this creation

You put the heat into the sun
You placed a heart in everyone

And all the music played and all the dancing done
Reminds us that we're made to be creative like

Creator God . . .[2]

There are countless other thematic ideas that will unite the generations. We all need to know we are fathered by a loving God, no matter how big or small; we all need to know God's presence in the night, whether that's because we're lying awake anxious or we've had a nightmare; we all need to be reminded of God's purposes for our lives, whether we are thinking about what we want to be when we grow up or whether we are retired and wondering what's next. The lyrical writing of these concepts obviously has to be carefully crafted so that all can understand and participate, but there is so much scope for the song themes to be key tools for bringing unity into our times of worship.[3]

2 Melody
We've already mentioned the need to have musical variety, but giving thought to the actual melody is also key. In recent years, one of the films that our whole family has loved together is *The Greatest Showman*. Each song seemed to pull at our hearts and impact us. We first watched it together when our youngest was three years old and our oldest was ten. It wasn't long before we all knew the lyrics to virtually every track and car journeys became predictable as once again the film soundtrack would be blaring out of the speakers. Somehow these songs stirred the hearts of every age in our family. The slow ballads were poignant and moving; the fast and full sound of some of the other tracks made us all want to dance. The melodies were singable but not dull or predictable.

In line with one of our core values—to give the same level of excellence to intergenerational worship as adult worship receives—we believe that church music for all ages can be just as powerful and sophisticated as the secular music being made in the world. For any budding songwriters reading this, write creatively for intergenerational sung worship! We need to get away from the old-school Bible songs 'for kids' and move towards melodies that engage our hearts as well as our minds and make the whole family want to blare the music out of the car speakers and sing along.

With every song we've written we've tried to deploy this value, and we aim for excellence in every area of the process, from writing to recording to lyric videos that help resource intergenerational worship. When we released the Worship for Everyone song 'Slingshot' in 2020, we felt we were really starting to push the boundaries of what can be possible for everyone. The song is contemporary, with production every bit as good as any other song released that year, and it tells the well-known story of David and Goliath but creatively interprets it as a metaphor for the power of God in us no matter what age and stage we are. The song has a rap in the middle too, which over the course of the year was learnt by many children (and adults!) around the country. I, Becky, used it in my school chapel to enable a 'rap-off' competition where hundreds of children competed, bringing a certain attitude and strength into their worship. At the same time, we were thrilled to receive a video of an elderly gentleman reciting the rap in his own home during the COVID lockdown!

It's exciting to find new and fresh melodies and styles of music that can engage and excite everyone. You may not be able to write the songs, but you can work hard at seeking out the resources you need to do intergenerational worship with skill and creatively. Don't settle for average or poor songs.

3 Storytelling and praise

When we began writing songs for intergenerational worship, we observed that traditionally many children's songs sang about

God or served to teach children about the Bible. There's nothing wrong with this, especially when we are talking about building a variety of all-age songs in our repertoires. However, if we solely concentrate on teaching children through songs, we risk missing the opportunity to disciple our children in releasing their hearts to God face to face. Ultimately, worship is about singing *to* God rather than *about* him.

As we've written over the years, we have intentionally tried to create a mixture of storytelling and praise. 'All Through History'[4] is a prime example of this:

> *Noah built the most enormous boat*
> *It kept the birds and animals afloat*
> *The Lord was good, the Lord was strong*
> *And Noah lived his life for him.*

Every verse teaches about God's faithfulness to his people throughout the Bible, moving from Noah and Moses to David and Daniel and then to Jesus. This would definitely fit the category of 'storytelling' or 'teaching'. But crucially, the choruses then sing out *to* God directly, thanking him that all through history he has been faithful:

> *Thank you, oh thank you*
> *That all through history you were faithful*
> *Thank you, oh thank you*
> *That you are just the same when it comes to me,*
>   *when it comes to me*

Another of our songs, 'God Is Love', similarly recites Jesus' command to 'love the Lord your God with all your heart, with all your soul and with all your mind' but then turns towards God in the chorus to simply declare 'God, we love you! That is why we sing!' So, where you can, remember to find a balance of storytelling and praise in your choice of songs.

4 **Emotions**

Linked again to variety, we have aimed across the years to include a wide scope of emotions in our songwriting. No matter what age and stage, we are human beings full of emotion. So often as we come face to face with God these feelings surface, which provides a great opportunity for God in our times of worship to pour out his healing, strength and encouragement. If we neglect to acknowledge or give space for our emotional life in our times together, we miss the chance to connect heart to heart with our Father and receive the fullness of life that he wants to pour into our tiredness or loneliness or anxiety. Equally if our songs neglect joy and praise and are too inward looking, we miss the chance to take our eyes off our own suffering and remember the triumph and victory of Jesus, which brings courage and perspective. Again, we need breadth and depth.

5 **Actions**

In the next chapter we talk more about actions, but in looking at your bank of songs for all ages, it's really worth making sure there are a variety of action songs. Actions are very important to help engagement, especially with younger children. We'll state our case for this later on.

These five categories help to distinguish songs that will work with everyone from those that might sit better in a more specific age-and-stage setting. If you're responsible for the catalogue of songs in your church, you may want to highlight the ones that tick the majority of these boxes and consider these the beginnings of an intergenerational song list. It might be that in looking through this checklist, you realise that you need to go and find a bunch of new songs! You can find all of our resources at worshipforeveryone.com or connect with our community at facebook.com/worshipforeveryone. A full thematic catalogue of the songs can be found in Appendix 3. If all the songs you currently use in an intergenerational gathering are upbeat dance songs, you might need some more reflective numbers that will bring musical and emotional variety. If everything you sing serves to teach the children and tell stories, you might need to seek out some more heart-to-heart praise songs. If all your themes tend to focus on Jesus, you might need some wider themes that look at God as Father or Creator, or at the power of the Holy Spirit, for example. The questions at the end of this chapter will help you decide what the next steps are in terms of song selection and use.

Finally, go for variety!

As you build your collection of intergenerational songs, ensure you have a good level of variety. Times of sung worship can easily get locked into a similar look and feel each week. What we've observed is that generally churches that are working hard to do intergenerational worship tend to get stuck in something fun and quite upbeat. They don't often journey beyond that to styles of singing that help to connect a child with their emotions, their questions and God's intimate presence by the Holy Spirit. Many churches that use contemporary worship are good at moving with the times but stay stuck with the one or two all-age songs that have 'worked' for twenty years—or more. Are you a church that values joy and praise? Then go big on joy and praise, but don't neglect reflection and intimacy, or the ministry of the Holy Spirit in worship. Children need time to pause in God's presence, just as we do. If you love words and theology, then train up your children that way too! But don't neglect to include a few simple songs that they can easily memorise and sing without effort, songs that will release heart response. Variety will help to meet many different needs across your congregation and disciple your people to discover that we can bring all we are in every season to God—our joy and sorrow, our fun and serious sides, our dance and our contemplation, our shouts and our whispers.

Crafting an intergenerational time of sung worship

We mentioned earlier that one of our goals in leading sung worship is to take the congregation on a journey from revelation to response. The beginning of our time together focusses on who God is. Then when our minds have focussed on God's attributes, our hearts naturally open up and respond to his goodness and love. It's no different when children are in the room. We want to help them on the same journey towards an encounter with the risen Jesus and the work of the Holy Spirit through how we craft the songs flowing together.

In case, like us, you have the opportunity to lead a time of sung worship with your whole church, it might help to outline how we would go about preparing this. Here is an example of a song list we have used in the past, with our reasons for selecting these pieces. The songs are from our own collection unless stated otherwise.

Worship song list and flow

1 **'Big Family of God':** This serves so many purposes and is a great choice for an opener. It focusses on God's unconditional love. It also reminds us that he's a Father and we are part of his family. It immediately says to the full congregation, 'You belong here! You are loved by God!', so it also communicates the Worship for Everyone vision from the outset. The actions create a sense of unity among everyone.

2 **'God Is Love':** This continues the theme of God's love, teaching Jesus' central command to love God with all we've got, but the chorus releases praise by singing out our love directly to God. It provides a good flow thematically from the first song but encourages all to move towards heart-to-heart praise. The actions in the chorus are so worshipful and simple that adults are totally happy to engage as well; we always find it brings a real sense of togetherness in worship and God's presence with us as we worship.

3 **'King of My Heart'[5] (chorus only):** This is one of our favourite choruses for singing with children present. Here we take the music level down and just start simply singing, 'You're never gonna let me down.' We often ask the children to first sing over the adults and then swap parts. It's incredibly powerful. Then we come together singing, 'You are good!' This can naturally segue into a prayer led by a child or a child and an older member of the congregation, and then we end the sung worship. Or if there's time for another song . . .

4 **'Every Step':** This is a good song to move into next as it is simple and repetitive, so not too jarring after the quieter moment of intimacy we've just had, but the pace picks up slightly, bringing everyone back together to finish. It continues to remind everyone of God's presence with us, and again we sing over one another that God is with us every step we go, so it serves as an encouragement to the body. The song is set to sign language, so the actions are beautiful and very inclusive for an older congregation. The feel is upbeat and positive, ending the time on a note of joy

and the hope that comes from staying close to Jesus and following his ways.

Obviously the specific song examples we've given may go out of date, but the principles behind our choices will help guide you regardless. They hopefully illustrate something of the importance of choosing songs carefully, working out a lyrical and musical flow and thinking ahead of time about when a moment for intimacy or 'pressing in' may fall. Having expectation *in advance* of what God may do, and having faith that God will be at work in the midst of the congregation no matter what our outward eyes see, is so important.

The power of intergenerational praise

It seems fitting to end with a story that shows the power of Worship for Everyone and what can happen through preparation, prayer and expectation when we select and use the right songs for everyone to worship:

One amazing full circle in my life was when a decade ago we got a phone call asking us to start to lead all-age celebrations at Spring Harvest. To think of all those times I'd snuggled up in my parents' arms enjoying worship in the Big Top at Skegness; it would've been a dream to imagine God would bring me back there one day to lead.

It was 2011, and we had taught one of our new songs, 'Faith', that week to the crowds in Butlins. It's a simple song reminding us that nothing is impossible for God and all we need is a tiny seed of faith. About three days in, we used this song as an opportunity for intergenerational groups to pray together and bring God their 'mountains' or battles. We handed out sheets of paper that were cut in the shapes of bricks (representing a wall of opposition to God's kingdom coming) and invited people from the littlest to the biggest to write down the areas of their lives where they were longing for breakthrough. We then invited the children to bring forward the bricks of prayer from their groups and lay them on the floor as we sang over these seemingly immovable obstacles. It became a very powerful time of worship, as unprompted and spontaneously children began to dance on the bricks, and then some started tearing them up and flinging them all over the room in tiny bits—it felt moving and prophetic whilst also a bit 'on the edge of chaos' and messy!

The week ended and we returned home, only to receive an email several days later from a woman who had been in the venue that evening and wanted to share her story with us. She told us how she had suffered for a long time with ME and even at Spring Harvest had struggled to make many of the sessions. She had virtually dragged herself into our session that particular night, together with her husband and four children, and during the worship time her family had written 'Mum's health' on a prayer 'brick' piece of paper. She had watched as the children danced at the front all over the bricks and tore them up, spreading them around the room. She had gone to bed that night feeling much the same but, to her surprise, woke the next morning feeling entirely different. She had energy for the first time in months and went on to enjoy a full day with her family. She went home wondering if it was a momentary high, but a week on, at the time of writing, she was still feeling completely different from how she had been before Spring Harvest. She put it down to the prayer that had been prayed as we worshipped that night.

The story gets better, as amazingly she wrote to us again six months later wanting to update us, and wonderfully she said she now felt consistently well again. All her chronic fatigue had lifted and she was enjoying a normal life with her family, praise God!

Now, there are of course countless stories of God healing people at conferences and during ministry time, but we share this story here because it is an example of all ages witnessing and enjoying the power and life of God together in worship. This miracle could have happened in the Big Top 'adult worship' without children present. This miracle could have happened during a Sunday local church service, when the woman's children would perhaps have been in their kids' groups. But God chose to heal her when her children were singing and interceding for her in the room. The entire family, as well as the big family of God present (including many single stewards, who loved engaging in the worship times despite their role to merely steward the venue!), got to share in her healing together. This is surely the goal of intergenerational worship done in Spirit and truth: Worship for Everyone!

Importantly, if you'd been in the room with us that evening, you'd have seen a fun, upbeat praise song with actions. You might have thought that nothing particularly special was happening. But playing that song were a team of people who had prayed for the power of God to be at work in just the same way that they'd have prayed had they been leading a bunch of adults. You'd have heard a band of musicians playing songs that had been well planned and rehearsed, with skill. You'd have heard expectation and hope in their conversations before they led the meeting of what God might do that night. By 2011, five years into our journey of writing songs and leading intergenerational worship, we and our team had come to realise that God wants to reveal himself and move among his people when children and all ages are present, and we should expect no less. There is hope for our churches, but it starts with vision, faith and prayer!

Getting the songs right

Since we introduced Worship for Everyone's songs into our whole-school devotions around four years ago, there has been a shift in culture around our praise and worship. Quite honestly, my memories of singing hymns when I was at school are of lifeless songs and drab lyrics. Occasionally things were jazzed up with some actions and maybe a few snazzy piano chords, but nothing actually inspired me to think about what I was singing.

Worship for Everyone songs are a total contrast. The children sing with enthusiasm and the lyrics act as vehicles for talking about Jesus. When we teach the songs, we also teach what they mean in such a way that children and staff can own what they are singing. Younger children love using the actions to help them remember the songs, whilst the older children go deeper with the themes and enjoy the catchy melodies.

One thing I have loved to see is how staff, Christian and non-Christian alike, have embraced every Worship for Everyone song. It's amazing to see children and colleagues singing lyrics like 'Jesus living in us can change the world' at the top of their voices in the school hall on a Monday morning!

Jake Bateson
Lead practitioner at All Saints Multi-Academy Trust, Birmingham

Questions to consider

1 Do you have a list of songs that you typically sing when all ages are present? Is it simply a handful that you repeat a lot, or do you have a more significant catalogue?

2 What song or songs work best currently when the whole church is together and why do you think they work so well?

3 Do you focus on singing about God, or do your intergenerational worship times sing to God?

4 Do you have melodic and emotional variety throughout your songs, or do you feel stuck in one style?

5 What's the next step you need to take to broaden the scope of your all-age worship songs?

8

Actions—why use them?

How do you feel about action songs? We tend to find that they really divide people. In reality they divide me (Becky)! I've been in churches where as an adult I've been invited to spin around and bark like a dog for Jesus in the name of all-age worship and I've wanted to die. But I have also experienced the most powerful sense of unity as I've led a congregation in action songs that have worked across the ages.

Actions can be a key tool in facilitating intergenerational worship, as long as they are thoughtful and designed to unite, not alienate and divide further. Older people cannot spin around frantically, just as children can't understand the words in many hymns. Worship for Everyone needs to be carefully crafted to remove some of these kinds of barrier. Therefore, part of creating actions for worship is being mindful of everyone. Not every song needs to have actions, but when they do, make sure you know why and what you're trying to achieve with them. Here are some tips for using actions from our experience:

1 **Never do an action song without an action leader at the front**. Or, if you do, don't allow yourself to get frustrated if no one joins in! Actions are often hard to remember, especially if you're also trying to concentrate on reading words, so an action leader is as important as a worship leader. In fact, the action leader *is* a worship leader. Having someone at the front is also a great model for the church. It gives permission to the more cautious members to jump

in and invites everyone to participate. Ideally, have a small crowd of all ages leading! This can also be a great way to start releasing children in leadership and get them involved in serving and having purpose.

2 **Ensure that the action leaders, including any singers or band members who are joining in, know the actions inside out**. These leaders are crucially there to give confidence to the congregation. If they don't know what they're doing or make regular mistakes, it can be a huge distraction. Once you've assigned your leaders, encourage them to take their role as seriously as the musicians do. You may want to appoint an action co-ordinator who will meet and briefly rehearse with the action leaders before the service. When we are leading at conferences we have a daily action rehearsal, in the same way we would have a daily band practice. And our motto for leading actions is you have to 'go big or go home'! There's no halfway house. We encourage our leaders not to hold back or be shy, but to go out confidently and praise God with all they've got, leading the way for the rest of the church to follow. Confidence up front releases confidence in the congregation to join in. If the people at the front don't look like they know what they're doing, then the people in the chairs will not want to follow them. Simple!

3 **Make sure your church knows why you're doing action songs**. There will always be some people who find them excruciating or cringy, but it can be an enormous help—or even a complete mind-shift—to hear from someone the thinking behind using them. I have often explained to congregations that the Psalms call us to 'bow down', 'lift hands', 'clap' and 'shout'. Worship has always been physical! Actions are simply a way of *scripting our physical response,*

rather like how a songwriter provides us with words to sing. Again and again we have seen scripted actions help the less spontaneous to use their bodies in worship more comfortably. People who would never normally raise hands in worship suddenly do it because it's scripted to do it!

And so I often address the adults in the room before leading actions, directly asking them to participate, even if they feel a little awkward. In other words, I address the elephant in the room! I explain that this way, we can all unite together, even those who are too little to read. It's an invitation to the adults to 'honour' these little ones for a song or two and lay down our preferences to serve theirs.

On other occasions I have talked about the power of using our bodies and voices together to help us remember words and open us up to God. The synchronisation of our body movements and the lyrics forms deeper connection between the content of what we're singing and our whole being— mind, heart and body.

Don't be afraid to speak and lead like this outside the actual songs—just the odd sentence before a song can make a real difference to the level of participation. It says to people: 'I know what you're thinking, but I know what I'm doing and I have confidence in where we're going and why we're doing this. Trust me, come with me and see the power of God at work as we unite together.'

4 **Choose actions that will help *your* people**! You know your church family. Are there lots of youth, who would appreciate dance moves? Or do you have more preschoolers, who would engage better with simple, more traditional actions? What works for one church might not work for another—and don't forget, there is no copyright on actions, so you are free to tailor them to your church!

5 **Consider using sign language**. We have over the years used both British and American signs in some of our songs, and they tend to be easier for adults to access and worship to. There are numerous sites online that demonstrate the signs if you need help with this—just search for British Sign Language. There's a real beauty in bringing this language into our worship, and of course it's another way to make our worship more inclusive, as it draws in those with impaired hearing. You don't have to sign an entire song—in fact, that could be extremely challenging for the majority of the congregation. We sometimes pick one or two signs and weave them into a piece. Alternatively, just sign the chorus or another key section of a number. We have sometimes brought the music down very low or to silence and then led the whole congregation to sign the words together—it can be extremely powerful.

6 **Remember variety**. Not every all-age song has to have actions; you also might choose to put actions just in the verses and then encourage people to freely respond or clap along in the chorus. This is a good way to teach children about both scripted and spontaneous praise. 'God Is Love,' which we quote in the previous chapter, has some actions in the verses, but during the chorus we simply model raising our arms in worship. It's technically an action and forms part of the song, but it begins to feel more like spontaneous praise. It's an easy and powerful way to begin to get children (and adults!) used to lifting their arms to God in worship.

> **Testimony from a forty-two-year-old dad of three, London**
>
> I used to hate doing actions. Literally hated it. I found it embarrassing and awkward. I really didn't want to spend my Sunday morning looking

like a fool. It also stopped me ever wanting to invite a colleague from my job in the city to church. But for the sake of the kids—particularly my youngest—I would grit my teeth and try to look like I was enjoying myself. But something in me shifted after about three years at the church. It was Easter time and Nick and Becky were leading a song about the cross ('Sign Your Cross'). They had taught us all the actions, which included a bit of sign language and then some very simple motions centred around signing the cross. I'd grown up in a Catholic home, so it made a lot of sense to me, as this was actually a familiar action that Catholics regularly do as part of their everyday life. As the song played, the tempo was steady and thoughtful, and I realised I was watching an entire room of adults and children all singing and moving together. It felt very powerful. It felt like real worship. I looked at my children that day doing actions alongside me and it was the first time I felt proud to be joining with them in this beautiful song of praise, rather than wishing the whole thing would end. I guess I'm not saying I'm 100 per cent an action convert, but I do think now that if they are crafted with care, they can provide a very helpful and unifying way to worship as a whole church.

Questions to consider

1 Do you have designated action leaders in your church to lead from the front? If so, are they a range of ages? Would you benefit from assigning a co-ordinator and encouraging rehearsals?

2 Take a look at your bank of intergenerational songs. Are there any action songs that, instead of unifying, have the opposite effect? Do you need to drop any of these songs or redesign some actions?

3 How could you go about helping the congregation share your vision on the use of actions in worship?

9

Delivering an all-age talk

It's interesting how many gifted and experienced church leaders have admitted to us over the years that while they feel equipped to preach to adults, they are slightly terrified of giving a talk when children are also present. In ordination training in the Church of England, certainly the focus throughout is on ministering and speaking to adults. Very little thought or time is given to equipping our future leaders with tools for leading intergenerationally. Within the church we have become so accustomed to age-and-stage ministry that many leaders delegate the intergenerational talks to others in the congregation and don't challenge themselves to grow personally in this gift—in the same way that Nick and I, in our mid-twenties, felt equipped to lead adults in sung worship but didn't initially consider that we needed to stretch our skills to lead worship intergenerationally. If worship is for everyone, then preaching the word of God is for everyone too.

I've found as time has gone on that when I've been able to preach to a room of all ages and hold their attention, it is the most fulfilling experience. There are times I can hear a pin drop as children as little as four stare open-mouthed and grandparents are transfixed. With the help of the Holy Spirit and a lot of thorough preparation, I think it's possible, and very exciting, to engage, challenge and minister a sermon to all ages. In fact, they can be some of the most powerful talks you ever do. If you're uncertain, don't give up! Read on . . .

Tone

Before we move into some tips on how to prepare well, I want to begin with an important observation on tone. A good friend advised me some years ago that speaking to children in church is comparable to speaking to newcomers who are exploring faith. What does this mean? As a mother, I have learnt over time that children can take far more than we often give them credit for—and they are certainly fascinated with all the things we might instinctively want to protect them from. I've chosen to parent my children with as few secrets and taboos as possible. As a result, I can see in them a certain maturity and thoughtfulness that in part has arisen from the many conversations we have had about anything and everything.

In the same way, as we 'parent' the children in our church through teaching, I would suggest that our tone in all-age gatherings can be geared to the older child. Think of an eight-year-old rather than a three-year-old. Let's not talk down or condescend. It's still possible to engage the youngest with a few handy tips! But if we think about speaking to a newcomer exploring faith, we will keep our words jargon-free and explain concepts clearly, assuming no previous knowledge. This will, for the most part, communicate to children as well. But additionally, we won't fall into the trap of ignoring the adults. On the contrary, they will hopefully feel included and find something that they too can connect with or feel challenged by.

How to prepare

1 **Write towards a response:** Be clear on what you want everyone to take away before you even start writing. For example, on Fathers' Day at our church we wanted the congregation to feel united around the fact that each of

them has been adopted by our heavenly Father. We didn't want anyone to feel that they couldn't participate in this day. Regardless of how they viewed their earthly fathers, today was relevant for everyone in the room, as 'we have all been adopted into one family'. I knew the response before I had planned the body of the talk. We were all going to write Fathers' Day cards to God and then put them on the stage as offerings of worship. The talk was geared to the response.

2 **Keep it simple:** We are used to three-point sermons or even five-point sermons. But an all-age talk is a one-point sermon! I think that's why they are often far more memorable than other talks. Choose the one point you want to make and find several ways of saying it. For example, a recent gathering I spoke at was on the theme of mission, and we used the title 'Show-and-Tell' as a way of demonstrating how we are to live as Christians. My entire talk was based on this one point—we are called to 'show-and-tell Jesus'. So, I brought my own show-and-tell, the Bible passage included verses on how we show and tell (Col. 4.2–6) and I gave a story of a time I had witnessed someone both showing and telling Jesus. I reiterated the phrase again and again. Keep it simple and it will be remembered for a long time!

3 **Keep it short:** We aim for seven minutes. I know it might sound very short, but you can communicate your one point well in that time. Any more and you will lose the little ones, which means you will also lose their parents. If you leave the people wanting more, it's no bad thing! Concentration spans will be varied across the room, so definitely don't go over ten minutes. This will also help you to stay focussed on that one point.

4 **Stories:** Stories help to keep attention and can bring theology to life in a really powerful way. Jesus was a storyteller. He would often have been speaking to crowds with children present. If you can include a story or two in your talk, you will have an easier time engaging everyone. I often talk about real people and real things that have happened to me. I find that I can talk most fluently that way, and inevitably that makes my communication more alive. I remember talking in my school chapel to 300 children and teachers about a girl who didn't like me when I was at school. I was totally open about what she did and how that made me feel. I didn't shy away from being vulnerable and honest. I could feel complete attention in the room from all ages: fascination from pupils who had visited me to talk privately about cases of bullying or friendship problems they'd had, and equal fascination from colleagues who were getting to know me a bit more. By telling personal stories where we can, we allow others to relate and children to realise that they're not alone—grown-ups have been there too, and survived, and found comfort from God or transformation in the process. Stories are so powerful, so do use them! At least one story in the talk is a must.

5 **Be visual:** Try to include at least one visual element. This could be a prop, a movie clip or simply a picture on the screen. Many people are visual learners, and it will also help to break up the speaking and once again hold the attention of the younger ones in the room.

6 **Use children:** Children love to see other children on the stage. It will immediately grab their attention if there's a chance they might be selected—particularly if there's the possibility of a prize thrown in! Wherever I can, I find a

reason to have a volunteer or two. It's helpful to break up a talk by having a bit of crowd interaction in the middle, just as attention might be waning with the little ones.

7 **Be creative:** Think outside the box. There are so many ways to communicate, alongside the words we use. I've seen people create dance routines, use exercise bikes, run games, even tape kazoos under everyone's chair! The purpose of the talk is to communicate the Bible in a relevant, meaningful and memorable way, so be free in how you choose to do that.

It may be that as you think about your intergenerational services, there are congregation members who would be really gifted at delivering an all-age talk but wouldn't necessarily be a first choice for an 'adult only' talk! We've had church members who would struggle to teach an in-depth series on Romans to the church, but their personal Bible knowledge, good communication skills and love of God equips them perfectly to give a five-minute talk to an intergenerational congregation. Think about where the skills and passion for all-age ministry lie—you might find some hidden gems in your church family. It's worth looking with fresh eyes at your preaching rota. If you're a church leader, make sure you are on that rota too!

A good talk makes a huge difference to how the overall service *feels* to everyone who has come. If we're brutally honest with ourselves, so many all-age talks in church are merely suffered by our congregations, rather than attentively engaged with and transformative. Let's not settle for average in our preparation and delivery for intergenerational services, but press on towards skilfully, creatively communicating the good news, as Jesus himself did.

Questions to consider

1 How do you feel about speaking to all ages? Do you feel skilled or ill equipped? Confident or nervous?

2 Spend a moment analysing the length and style of your church's current all-age talks. Is there anything you would change, having read this chapter?

3 Do all ages tend to listen and concentrate when someone speaks? What could promote further engagement in your context?

4 Are there congregation members you could add to your speaking rota? If not, are there people you can identify to train up?

5 What's the next step for your context?

10

Constructing an all-age service

Having looked at some of the elements that go into leading intergenerational worship, we're now going to look at how to bring these elements together in a well-crafted service. What are some of the principles that, if followed, can make a big difference to engaging all ages in worship? Is it even possible?

Understanding church as family

I, Becky, am writing this at Christmas time—so, by way of example, think of a Christmas mealtime in a large family gathering. Grandma is maybe pulling a cracker with her seven-year-old grandson, while Grandad is making sure the wine glasses are topped up and Dad is telling a terrible joke (obviously). Mum is nursing the baby and eating one-handed, while a friend of the family is helping to chop up the four-year-old's Brussels sprouts and everyone is laughing (or groaning at the punchline!). This is a picture of messy harmony. It's a picture of all ages working together—one serving the other, and all opting to partake in the silly party hats, despite the fact the grown-ups would never do it at a grown-up dinner party. And the children are on best behaviour because the family friend is there and it's Christmas Day, and they want to behave politely in front of Grandma.

This is a good image of church when intergenerational worship is fully functioning. It provokes us not to ask of our services 'Is everyone happy?', but instead perhaps to ask, 'Is everyone loving the other? Serving one another? Working as one body? Acting as a family—the big family of God?'

There's a great principle found in the book of Romans, chapter 12, verse 10: 'Be devoted to one another in love. Honour one another above yourselves' (NIV). In the current climate, we are so programmed to be individualistic that we can easily slip into judging church by how much we get out of it personally and by how much our own needs are met. But the Bible tells us that we need to honour one another *above* ourselves. Think back to that Christmas dinnertime. Yes, the mum could've left the baby crying for his food while she enjoyed her meal, Grandad could've poured his own wine and left the others to fend for themselves. The grown-ups could've refused to put the party hats on, and the children could've refused to sit at the boring old table and stayed watching TV, but how much would they have missed out on? A healthy, functioning family means give and take and honouring one another (or, in another translation, 'preferring' one another).

In our times of intergenerational worship the end goal isn't a roast dinner (although that would be nice!). The end goal is that everyone present can join with their wider spiritual family in enjoying God together. And if part of loving God is loving one another, this very act of being together *becomes* part of our worship to God the Father. True worship doesn't just begin when we start singing together but when we *choose to be together despite what divides us* (in this case, age and stage). Church services just for adults can reinforce our individualistic, self-serving bubbles. Intergenerational church forces us into more sacrificial levels of love, and therefore further into the heart of God.

So let's get practical! With all this in mind, let's think about constructing an intergenerational service that can help all the generations to come together in messy harmony.

A few golden rules from our experience:[1]

1 **Timing:** Create a service that is fifty to sixty minutes long. No one has ever complained about being sent home from church too soon! If you leave people wanting more, then you've really cracked it. They will start looking forward to the next one rather than dreading the all-age service. By keeping it short you will also help to keep the attention of the youngest members of the church—which in turn will help their parents to leave less stressed and feeling it was good to be there. We actually aim at fifty minutes in the planning of the service, as usually that will mean fifty-five to sixty in reality.

2 **Team:** Get a team in place and start planning well in advance. As mentioned in an earlier chapter, in our context we're blessed to have a large team, and so we sit down with the children's pastor, youth pastor and worship pastor several weeks before a service to start brainstorming the theme. If your church doesn't have these paid roles, try to gather the lay equivalent or some passionate volunteers.

3 **Theme:** The theme you decide upon needs to remain in sharp focus throughout the whole service. Every element should support the theme. You might base the theme on something seasonal that's happening, such as Palm Sunday, and then find the scripture that will form the foundation for it, or you might start with a more general Christian theme and draw out the key word or words you want to focus on, such as *hope* or *prayer*. Work out at this point what the goal of the service is, and from there you can start planning what you want the response to be. We do a lot of 'digging in' to the theology at this point. Basically the big question is 'What do we want everyone to take away from this?' and therefore 'Will each element of the service take us closer to

this goal?' A test in the planning process is always to ask yourself: Can I say in one sentence what the take-away is?

4 **Opening:** Have a strong welcome once the service starts. This service, more than any other, needs to give confidence to everyone from the outset. This is absolutely critical. The opening sentences, both in content and delivery, need to be positive, audible and invitational. Explain what's going to happen so everyone feels safe, and if it feels right, use the chance to rehearse the vision again, the 'why' of what we're about to do.[2] Just the odd line like 'It's so special to have times when we can all worship God together, no matter what age or stage of life you are at. We believe there is such a power when we unite together to worship him!' might be enough to switch a slightly reluctant adult on. Or we can remind our church, 'We have so much to learn from our little ones. Jesus said our faith needs to be more like a child's, so let's watch and learn!'

5 **Singing:** Choose the worship songs with care and attention. Some helpful thoughts and questions to ask are: Have I got a variety of song styles and dynamics? Do they support the theme where possible? Are the songs simple enough for children to join in? Is there enough musical interest for the adults? Do the songs lend themselves to actions? Do the songs facilitate true *worship* for everyone in the room? See Chapter 8 for more on forming a set of songs.

6 **Extra element:** Think about an interactive element that will release some joy or intrigue in the room. You probably only need one. It can be tempting to throw loads of 'fun' ideas into a service with children present, but in reality one brilliant quiz (*for everyone!*), or game, or drama, or YouTube clip might be all you need. The key thing is that this extra

element, whatever it is, should totally support or open up the theme. So, if you're doing a talk on Jesus as the light of the world, you could have a game of 'name that tune' where every answer contains the word *light*; if your theme is 'God as Father', you might have a film clip about a dad and their child or get a few actors in the church to dramatise the story of the Prodigal Son; if it's Palm Sunday, you might get two families to have a palm sundae-making contest! The more that everything points to the theme and reinforces your key message, the more memorable and meaningful these services will be. Sometimes less is more—and this way you'll begin creating services that are more sustainable to run. Focussing on one creative element means you'll hopefully dedicate some proper time to finding just the right thing! This extra element is usually good early on in the order to help set up the question you'll be answering in the talk.

7 **Readings:** Prayers and Bible readings provide two great opportunities to get other ages involved. An older member of the church might enjoy reading; a young family could write some prayers together and lead them or even record them in advance so there's a video element and something that shows people in their own environment. You might like to look at child-friendly Bibles for different versions of readings. *The Jesus Storybook Bible* by Sally Lloyd-Jones is a firm favourite of ours.[3] It is beautifully written, deeply spiritual for adults and yet very accessible for younger readers. One tip is to experiment with different ways of communicating the Bible. If there's a gifted storyteller in the church, you could ask them to paraphrase a story, or you could use YouTube to show an animated retelling of a story. Bringing the Bible to life for children in a relevant way will keep them engaged and interested in what they are hearing.

8 **Response:** The response is everything (virtually!) in our view. Leading people to a place where they can make their own personal response to God is what we as leaders are aiming for. One of my favourite Worship for Everyone services that I have run both in church and in my school is on Jesus' teaching in Matthew 6, where he tells the crowd how the Father sees what we do in secret and rewards us. The theme for this particular service was 'secret spy', and everything led to a response where I produced an enormous 'TOP SECRET' brown envelope and everyone was invited to write down one way they were secretly going to be a blessing to someone that week, 'for God's eyes only'. No one was allowed to tell anyone else, and the envelope was sealed. There was something very powerful about seeing everyone bring their secret blessing forward as we worshipped and knowing that all around the city that week acts of kindness would be carried out, purely for the applause of our Heavenly Father. In advance, carefully think and pray through precisely how the talk is going to land and what you're going to push into and invite for a response.

9 **Surprise:** Try to have a moment of surprise as a final little twist! I think there's something so special about surprising everyone. In my chapel at school, one of my goals is simply that the children and staff never quite know what is going to happen each week. It brings a sense of expectation; it sets the tone for what God often does— by his Holy Spirit we are often taken by surprise! I've had prizes sellotaped under chairs only to be discovered at a certain key moment; I've had a baby alpaca hiding behind the chapel, waiting for a grand entrance; I've had teachers appear in fancy dress and even a flash mob. It doesn't have to be as grand as this—even when, in our

home church, we've a reading done from the back of the building rather than the stage, it's a moment of surprise, something different to listen for, and it keeps the energy and expectation high.

10 **End well:** If you can, end on a note of joy, of praise, of celebration. Very simply, this can be done by choosing an up-tempo praise song which everyone can have fun and sing to ('Every Eye Is on You' is one of our favourites to use).[4] Equally, it can be more involved, such as giving out 'screamer balloons' and having everyone let them go together (we did this for a big Pentecost celebration) or kicking giant balloons into the congregation to try to keep up in the air as we sang the last song! Every service doesn't have to end like this, but it's a good baseline to do so. Sometimes, instead, we've ended quietly and in ministry time—children teaming up with a trained supervisor and joining in praying for people that the Holy Spirit would fill them afresh.

These are some of the tips for constructing a Worship for Everyone gathering. By way of example, here is a rough plan of an actual service we did in Gas Street, Birmingham. The script is included in the appendices.

Outline of a Worship for Everyone gathering with rough timings

Service theme and title: SHOW-AND-TELL

Aim

That all would be challenged to act and speak as Jesus would— both showing and telling him to the world.

Welcome

Welcome everyone and reinforce the vision of why intergenerational worship is so important. Set the theme, explaining that we are going to look at how God wants us to both show and tell Jesus in our lives. Open in prayer. **(Five minutes)**

Sung worship

A set of two action songs, and a chorus. **(Twelve minutes)**

'Creator God' (draw out how God has shown himself and speaks to the world through creation);

'God Is Love' (releasing worship with its simple chorus and reminding us that loving God is the chief goal for our lives);

Chorus of 'The Stand (Hillsong)', flowing from the end of 'God Is Love'—heart response to God's love;

Linger musically and have some space before praying to close the worship time. Segue into the next moment.

Drama

A bell rings offstage (sound effect).

A classroom teacher announces it's time for show-and-tell. Various children bring quirky or unusual items and say a couple of sentences about them. The final child is holding nothing, but when a puzzled teacher enquires about this, the child replies that he himself is the show-and-tell. (Full script in the Appendix 2) **(Five minutes)**

Reading

A child reads Colossians 4.2–6 (words on screen too):

2 Devote yourselves to prayer, being watchful and thankful. **3** And pray for us, too, that God may open a door for our message, so that we may proclaim the mystery of Christ, for which I am in chains. **4** Pray that I may proclaim it clearly, as I should. **5** Be wise in the way you act towards outsiders; make the most of every opportunity. **6** Let your conversation be always full of grace, seasoned with salt, so that you may know how to answer everyone. (**Two minutes**)

Notices and collection

We often send a bucket of sweets around with the collections. It's a little pick-me-up at the halfway point, and not just for the kids—make sure you put enough in *for everyone*! Sometimes we've tied the sweets into the theme—we've given out Parma Violets on Palm Sunday, Love Hearts on Valentine's Day and chocolate coins at Christmas. (**Five minutes**)

Talk

Summarised, in brief:

1 The speaker brings their own show-and-tell. Make it funny/quirky/something that has a story attached to it.

2 Explain the Bible verses, using actions for 'full of grace', 'seasoned with salt', etc. to help everyone memorise it.

3 Tell a real-life story of someone who has 'shown' the gospel in how they have acted or spoken. (**Eight minutes**)

Response

While the band plays gentle music, explain that you want every-one to take a quiet moment to think about someone this week to whom they would like to show and tell God's love. There are then various alternative ways you can lead the response:

1 Invite the church to tell the person next to them or tell their family who this is, and together commit this person to God in prayer. They can then take time to pray for each other to be filled with courage and love as they go. This involves children and adults ministering together.

2 Invite everyone to stand, then say a prayer over them, committing the people they have thought of to God. You can pray from the front that they will be filled with love and courage to show and tell Jesus. This involves the service leader ministering over the congregation, which may feel more comfortable for your people. You know your crowd, so adapt the approach accordingly!

3 Invite everyone to write on a piece of paper one way they would like to show and tell Jesus in the week ahead. They could bring these forward to the front and lay them down during worship, or take them home and keep them in a Bible. **(Seven minutes)**

Prayers

Invite an individual or family to come and pray over the response. **(Two minutes)**

Worship song

'City on a Hill', or another missionally themed song to end **(five minutes)**. We have used little LED lights or glow sticks at times when we've led this song as a visual reminder that we are called to be lights in the world. It also could be a nice surprise moment to hand them out at the end!

In summary, the components of every service for us include a welcome, worship time, an interactive moment (in the case above, it was a drama, but this could be a slot for a quiz or film clip), Bible reading, notices and collection, talk, response, prayers and final worship song, with a sharp theme that leads to a clear response running throughout. This is by no means prescriptive and we will sometimes move things around, but generally speaking we've found that this is a helpful structure. Your context and congregation will be different to ours, but keeping it simple, sticking to some of these key principles and doing the basics well will give you a good foundation to build on as you experiment yourselves.

Questions to consider

1 Think about each of the components above: timing, team, theme, opening, singing, readings, talk, response, surprise. In light of what you've read, is there anything you'd add to or take out of your current intergenerational services?

2 Did anything immediately challenge you? Are there any current practices that you want to change?

3 What's the best all-age service you've ever been a part of? What made it so good?

4 What's the next step for you in creating an intergenerational service based on these principles/ guidelines?

11

Delivering Worship
For Everyone online

Until 2020, here in the UK, the idea of 'doing' church online was occasionally debated theologically (ironically, often online): the pros and cons, the opportunities and the challenges. For most churches, especially small and medium-sized churches, it felt either totally irrelevant as a concept or perhaps like something to dabble in every now and then with a video posted of a sermon and maybe a community Facebook page. As has now been widely documented, the coronavirus pandemic has led to an acceleration of existing trends in all kinds of areas of society and technology—one of them being church online. Suddenly, online worship options and presence went from an optional extra for churches to an absolute necessity. It was a steep learning curve.

This shift to online spaces looks certain to be not only an enforced temporary necessity but also a positive long-term adaptation towards serving people who either may not want to attend church in person yet (providing them a safe window into what happens 'in' church) or are not able to attend physically due to health or accessibility issues. It seems likely to settle into an addition or supplementary partner to physical gathering and engagement.

One of the key shifts that happened due to the pandemic in an accelerated period of time was that the boundaries that appear in everyday 'normal life' for families between church, home and school suddenly came down. Everything became all-age, as everything was happening in the same place and everyone was there together.

During 2020, in our household, we knew we couldn't help on the frontline of the fight against the virus—working in hospitals, serving in supermarkets, etc.—but what we could do was beam some simple worship, teaching and prayer from our home into other peoples' homes. So a day or two after the first national lockdown was announced, we launched *Family at Four*—a thirty-minute Facebook Live show delivered by our whole family from a small room in our house. We didn't know what to expect with that first show; we didn't even know if the Internet would hold up and the camera work, never mind if Levi, our littlest child, would stay in the room for longer than a few minutes!

That first show felt messy, slightly chaotic, definitely stressful, but everything worked. For the next forty-eight hours, our phones didn't stop beeping with notifications. In the end, that first episode was viewed over 50,000 times. We couldn't believe the connections we had made and how relatively easy it had been for us to bless so many households in that thirty minutes.

Katy, age forty-one

Weekends were unusually very quiet for me during lockdown. A friend of mine shared a video of the first *Family at Four*. I thought I would give it a go and was instantly hooked. I really missed being with my church family. I always looked forward to *Family at Four*—an extremely fun, manic (in a good way), crazy and happy time. Just how my life was in normal times! It was very inclusive for everyone, whether part of a family or single and whether you were one or 100. It's amazing how one family on a TV screen made you feel like you were not on your own and could even get you singing and dancing round your living room! I felt very much a 'part of the big family of God'.

We had of course worked hard behind the scenes beforehand. As you would expect, having read the book up to this point, we had valued 'excellence' in some way—in this case making sure the video quality, the sound quality and the overall look and feel were good (which we define as 'the best you can do with the equipment and money you have'). We had researched online streaming software and invested in one to use. We'd thought through a theme, how each child would have a part to play, how we would work together interweaving the overall direction of the thirty minutes. We also thought of the importance of the people connecting in—we deliberately made it live so that it felt like we were literally in peoples' living rooms right there and then, all together in that moment, even though physically divided. We would comment on peoples' comments and interact via the camera.

Over the next nine months we went on to do three seasons of *Family at Four*—a total of thirty-one episodes reaching thousands of people of all ages each week across Facebook, YouTube and Instagram. It was an extraordinary season of uniting as the big family of God across the country and across the world as people of every age and stage from India, South Africa, Australia, Sweden and many other countries joined in to worship. It elevated children, it engaged adults and it displayed and offered the tremendous power of unity that we have been talking about throughout this book.

Mary Robins, retired schoolteacher

Whatever your situation—raising a family, single or elderly—*Family at Four* demonstrates ways a multifaceted melody of praise can lift God higher. How? Through genuine, spontaneous fun, the Drakes make the Bible come alive! Their laughter, drama, storytelling, interesting facts, prayers and music are so captivating that they always engage and give potential for extending themes to a greater level, no matter what age you are. Throughout this season of COVID-19, when corporate praise and worship during lockdown has been made so difficult, tuning into *Family at Four* on a weekly basis has brought light and hope into many lives.

For me, a retired schoolteacher without a family, I have loved every moment. It has been relevant, joyful and challenging. Above all else I feel I have now found my 'virtual' family and together we praise our wonderful Father.

We know there were some distinctions unique to us that made that season work particularly well (the fact we write our own songs and could use them easily without needing permissions, the fact we had six of us already locked down together—a ready-made team!). However, there are some general principles that are relevant for doing intergenerational worship online. We know that online ministry is here to stay; no matter what happens in the future, some form of hybrid church will be firmly established for upcoming generations. So it is important to be able to do it and do it well. Here's Becky with some general principles that we have learnt through our experience to help.

Helpful principles

As a mum, I have watched countless TV programmes and YouTube channels with our four children over the years. There are some shows I've endured and others I've genuinely enjoyed. Children's programmes such as *Blue Peter* and some of the Disney comedies have really drawn me in, and I've ended up laughing out loud at the humour or plot. Certain YouTube families have become much loved in our household because of their hilarious antics or close family dynamics.

Equally, I've been pleasantly surprised when one of my children has ended up gripped with me on a series I've watched for years. *Strictly Come Dancing* and *The Great British Bake Off* are examples of family shows where there's often broad appeal. We all love it in our household when we find a show like this that we can enjoy together.

So, when we come to creating online content that will connect the generations, it's worth considering what makes some of these shows so appealing to all. *Family at Four* was successful because somehow it appealed to two-year-olds, eleven-year-olds and seventy-year-olds. Here are a few tips for connecting online intergenerationally:

1 **Make sure the picture on the camera is sharp and in focus and the audio is clear.** No one will tune in for long if they can't see or hear what you're saying. Spend time getting the lighting right and ensuring your background is clean and not distracting. You may need to invest in some basic photography lights to help with this. An iPhone can be good enough quality if it is held in a tripod and the lighting is good. Otherwise (and ideally), use a high-quality digital camera as well as, crucially, a separate microphone.

2 **Bring energy and joy to the camera at the start.** It's hard to keep listening to someone who is monosyllabic or too serious or lengthy. Bring your most dynamic self. You may have to switch it on a bit if that feels unnatural! But remember you need to start well and grab people straight away. Once you've lost them, it's hard to get them back— especially children. Be clear in your first few sentences

about what this is, why anyone should watch it and what
will be coming up.

3 **Variety is crucial.** In a live gathering, people will focus on
the speaker at the front for a while, but they can also look
around the room, watch other peoples' responses and pick
up energy from laughter and smiles. Online, both the view
and the vibe are far more limited. So, bring variety where
you can. For example:

4 **Use props.** Holding up visual aids, toys, props—whatever
you can—will add colour and interest to what you're saying.
If you're telling the story of Moses, have a washing basket at
the ready. If you're talking about Noah, why not bring your
pet and introduce them to your church? Use whatever you
can at home to keep things looking and feeling interesting.

5 **Change location.** If the bulk of the content is coming from
one or two individuals, it's great to change up the location
if you can. If the talk is done in the lounge, could you do
some action songs in the garden or a craft activity in the
kitchen? Conversely, if you're mainly filming in a church
building, can there be something from a different context?
Or are you perhaps able to record something in advance
that you then slot into your final video? This adds energy
and variety, which will help to keep the viewers engaged.

6 **Don't talk endlessly.** Because the camera is so much more
one-dimensional than being live and present, limit how
long you talk for. If I allow myself seven to ten minutes to
preach to all ages live, I would stop myself at five minutes
on camera. I get cross with myself when I go on for much
longer! If that feels too hard, break up your talk into two

halves. Speak for three or four minutes, change to some different content—a song or activity, for example—and then do part two of the talk. Just keep the content moving as much as you can.

7 **Be natural.** The authentic you is the most engaging thing you can bring. But that doesn't necessarily mean winging it (unless you're a real pro!). In fact, from experience, those who look and sound the most natural are usually the ones who have worked hardest and prepped the most. Where possible, try not to read what you're saying. If you have to read it, rehearse it so well that you can look up a lot and remain engaged with those watching.

8 **Imagine you are speaking to a real human.** It's easy to present online like you're giving a speech in front of an anonymous room. But don't forget that you're communicating with your church family—people you know and love—so you can ask them how they are, smile and relate as if they are really there. It will help to communicate warmth and relationality and prevent the time feeling too sterile or formal.

9 **Involve all ages.** It's not always possible, but if you can have a wide variety of ages involved online, it adds so much. Children love watching children. Grandparents also love seeing children. I think Levi, our littlest, has become the most popular Drake in our online episodes! But equally, it's so valuable having one of our older congregation members praying for younger families, or finding a single professional who can pray for others in their workplaces, etc. Let's live out on screen the intergenerational value as much as we can.

10 **Stories work brilliantly online.** Everyone loves a good story! If you feel nervous about telling your own or going off the script, find a good children's Bible and read a story using props or costumes. I've found even popping a wig or hat on and pretending I'm a Bible character can be immediately entertaining and interesting.

11 **Remember the goal—everyone worshipping.** Whatever you're presenting online, know what your goal is and where you want to land. Plan a response and find something that everyone is going to take away. Are you going to lead into a time of quiet, reflective prayer at home? Are you going to give a challenge to do that week? Often in *Family at Four* we use household things to help families go away and pray. Popping a written prayer in a Tupperware box or drawing a picture over dinner together is simple and doesn't require people to go and buy any resources, but can help to extend the time of worship and bring further engagement after the service has ended.

Online church is here to stay in some way. It can be an excellent addition to on-site worship. If it's done well, it is a key missional tool for attracting families and individuals on the edge of Christianity and giving them a safe window into a faith community. It can also provide a connection point for families of children with special needs who struggle to cope in a live setting. And, as we found during lockdown, it can be a comfort to our ageing congregation, who equally may struggle some weeks to get to church but still long to feel connected to the big family of God. Who knows how the kingdom might begin to grow in new ways as our churches invest more in reaching all ages online in the future!

Questions to consider

1 If your church is currently engaging with people online, how do you feel it is going? What are some of the strengths and weaknesses of your current online services?

2 Who do you think is watching your current online content? Is it intergenerational or are there specific age groups you are prioritising?

3 How could you use this tool missionally in your context?

4 Based on some of the practical tips in this chapter, what steps do you need to take to improve your online content and further engage all ages with it?

12

Worship for schools

Much of this book is devoted to pursuing intergenerational worship in church settings, but I, Becky, have also had the privilege and experience of being an all-age practitioner in a school context. We may think of schools as purely child focussed, but as a school chaplain I would consider every service or assembly to be intergenerational. Children and teachers are present together, and throughout the calendar year in my school, parents will attend certain assemblies and chapel services. In the COVID era, we also developed new ways of working so that much of our content was recorded and viewed in the homes of our school families; this is something that will continue into the future, as it's become evident that parents love to see and hear what their children are doing, and in many ways it's so much easier communicating by video than expecting busy parents to take time out of work to come into school for everything. As we've seen in the previous chapter, the additional benefit of video is that it can be shared more broadly with wider family and friends and kept as a memory for the future. In addition to this, the songs we sing at school will end up being sung at home, so parents become part of what the children are learning and singing within their school day.

Church schools have such an important role to play in reinforcing all that's being taught at home and in church. If you're a school leader or church leader with access to your local primary school, your role is extremely significant in the lives of the children and families you're serving. There will be some children in your school for whom you are the only Christian voice in their lives. The missional opportunity and urgency of what you do and say to these children is immense! I have seen the Holy Spirit work in and through the children and teachers I serve in so many little ways—and sometimes in very significant and powerful ways. Be encouraged that if you have the privilege of working in a school, God wants to use you as a missionary in that place, not only in what you say or teach but in how you love and show the kindness of Jesus. I often feel like I'm a spiritual mum to hundreds in my school, with the opportunity to pour out love and encouragement to the children in my care. It is so needed and so important.

I have felt God say to me many times that the school work I've done over the years is the business of seed-sowing. I don't often expect to see the fruit of God's kingdom with my own eyes, but I have faith—and you can too—that all the little acts of love and the moments of teaching and worship that we do in school will have a far greater and more lasting impact than we will ever know! And sometimes we even get the privilege of seeing these moments unfold . . .

Singing with nursery and reception, London

For several terms when my children were little, I would volunteer to go into their school weekly to lead worship with nursery and reception children. As mentioned in Chapter 2, I had heard it said that 'there is no junior Holy Spirit', a phrase that had really stuck in my memory, so with this in mind I would pray each week that the same Holy Spirit in me would encounter the children before me.

In all honesty, time and again it felt like we had a lovely sing-song. I would play our tracks on a slightly ropey CD player and the children loved the actions and melodies, but did I honestly think I was having much spiritual impact? Probably not. I began to feel a little weary when each Friday came along and it was time for me to head over to the school. Then one afternoon, as I ended our song 'All Through History', which speaks of God's faithfulness and goodness to his people, I noticed a slight commotion at the back—a little boy was in tears. I assumed he'd hurt himself. I carried on speaking to the children until the teacher, a Christian woman, suddenly appeared at the front of the classroom, holding his hand. Having spoken to the boy, she explained to the classroom that he was crying because he suddenly felt that he really loved God and didn't know what to do. The faith-filled teacher asked if anyone would like to pray for him. My embarrassingly sceptical self couldn't imagine another four-year-old volunteering for the task! But I was proven wrong by the sweetest little boy, who stood up and confidently prayed, 'Thank you, God, for making the world and for making [the boy]. Thank you that you love all of us. Amen.' The Holy Spirit was so tangibly at work in the room. It was so evident that something special was happening. The teary boy had had no previous Christian experience or upbringing but had clearly encountered God through this simple, unsophisticated time of worship. God showed me that day the power of his spirit in weakness.

Several months later I bumped into the little boy and his mum outside the school gate. He stopped and said to me, 'Do you remember that thing that happened to me in class when you came to sing?' I said that I did remember and that I thought it had been a very special moment in his life. I had the chance to share with his mum that he had been very impacted by a worship song, and she was open and receptive as we spoke. Another small chance to sow a seed.

We have so much to learn from the faith of children in our midst. We can also have confidence in the small acts of service we offer. God is bigger than our gifts and our faith and can reach a child in an instant. He will always honour the faith we have and the time we give in serving him. So let's pray for fruit and impact in the lives of the children we serve!

I had no idea when I began volunteering in my children's school all those years ago that one day I would become a school chaplain and have the opportunity to spiritually input into the lives of hundreds of children and families. Some of what I've learnt along the way may be helpful to you if you're a teacher, school leader or parent volunteer.

The language we use in school

Much of what we have shared throughout this book will apply in schools as well as churches; however, your language will probably need nuancing a little. As mentioned in a previous chapter, my school's context is urban and multifaith, so I'm very careful about not alienating. I don't shy away from talking about Jesus, but I'm careful with my phrasing. Often I will say 'Christians believe that . . .' or 'the Bible tells us . . .' so that children of other faiths can still listen and learn without feeling uncomfortable or excluded. I also believe that all faiths can learn from Jesus whether or not they believe he is the son of God, so I will talk about his wisdom and incredible storytelling, which are indisputable regardless of a child's faith.

My brother, a head teacher in Bolton, Lancashire, leads a church school and says that in his view the language we use is a vital way to ensure inclusivity in the school community—both with children and with staff. He told me that he regularly introduces prayers by saying, 'I'm going to say a prayer, and if you like it, you can say "Amen" at the end, which means you agree and like the prayer. Or, if you'd prefer, you can just sit and think quietly about what we've spoken about today.' This ensures that all can participate in some way. He would say the vast majority join in, but by giving freedom, it means we're not making those of different faiths feel obliged to uncomfortably participate.

Whole-school values

The school I currently work in, like many others, has a set of four key values, which reflect the Christian faith and ethos of the school. Our four values are:

1 Be kind and patient

2 Show respect

3 Be truthful

4 Persevere

These are memorised by all children across the school. They appear on class walls, they are regularly taught about, and children receive stickers whenever they are spotted demonstrating one of the values. Every now and again I give a half-term to looking more deeply at one of the values and putting it in a Biblical context. For example, I gave six weeks to exploring kindness. I spent two weeks looking at being kind to ourselves, then two weeks on being kind to others and finally looked at being kind to the world. I used stories and verses from the Bible to show Jesus' kindness and God's love for us and the world. I taught the children that being like Jesus isn't just about being kind, it's about being EXTRA kind. This school value will not be forgotten in a hurry!

A head teacher's advice on worship in school . . .

As a head teacher who has led worship in a primary school setting for over fifteen years, my one biggest piece of advice is 'keep it simple'. This applies to everything from the theme over a period of time to the language used when you pray to the message of each worship session and to the songs chosen.

I always bear in mind that children and adults in a school setting are bombarded with messages every day. Every lesson has a new focus, children might have individual learning and behaviour targets and there might be issues at home for adults and children too. So I see worship as a time for all participants, and I like adults to attend worship as it's an opportunity to reinforce whole-school messages and values, to sit back and take some time out of their busyness to hear one clear, simple, important and relevant message. I like to start with a fun and apt way to introduce the topic, maybe using a puppet, watching a clip from a movie or telling a personal anecdote. I'll then draw out the point using a biblical story or message and focus it very firmly on the spiritual. I always have a reflection where I ask children to think about their response to the message, and I end with a prayer, using quite conversational language, showing children and staff that a prayer doesn't have to be formal or traditional—although there is definitely a time and a place to learn liturgical prayers, especially the Lord's Prayer. Songs that I use usually have familiar language and simple, straightforward, nonenergetic actions, allowing reception class children to join in and not making the older year-six children feel patronised. Songs like 'City on a Hill' and 'Big Family of God' are brilliant examples of this—simple language, simple actions and great melodies! Since introducing them in my school last term, I've heard adults and children alike humming them around school.

Where all-age worship works well, it's inclusive, it's relevant and it's firmly grounded in the Bible and Christian values—challenging staff and children alike to consider their ideas, thoughts and behaviour as we all try to become more like Jesus.

Matt Harding
Head teacher
St Peter's Smithills Dean Primary School, Bolton

Termly themes

I spend a lot of time planning the term ahead and having a consistent theme for either the half-term or full term. At times, I've taken just one word as a theme. For example, one term I looked at 'light'. Each week I unpacked a different element of God being light: creation, when God spoke light and life into the world; Moses and the fire that burned by night, showing light as direction; Jesus, the light of the world, as an image of power defeating the darkness; us being like a city on a hill, encouraging the children to shine with God's love to those around them.

Other times, I've taken some of Jesus' teachings, like the parables, the 'I am' statements or Beatitudes, and worked through them across the term. There are five ways each week that I try to reinforce the theme for that week. If you're a school leader, you may find some of this helpful:

1 **Thought for the week**
   Each Monday morning, the children watch a five-minute 'thought for the week' in their classrooms, recorded in advance. It's very simple. We use a school camera, but it

could just as easily be captured on and uploaded from a smartphone. This is where I set out the theme for that week. One term, for example, we looked at God's promises; each Monday of that term I shared the promise for that week— for example, 'I will never leave you or forsake you' and 'I will give you strength'—and then said a few words about it. Some weeks I told a Bible story that showed the promise in action, such as the story of David and Goliath proving God's strength in weakness or the story of Daniel in the lion's den as a sign of God's promise to protect us. The beauty of this short video is that it's easy to make and gives the children a strong focus at the start of the week and something to build on as the week continues. During COVID it was the only way our school could 'gather' together, as we weren't able to congregate for our usual whole-school worship. I record one for our infants and one for our juniors.

2 **Song of the week**
   Every week I have a worship song that ties in with our theme. I announce it in the thought for the week and then ask the class teachers to play it whenever they can in their classrooms. I use a lot of our Worship for Everyone songs but also introduce songs across many Christian genres, from gospel to contemporary. For our younger children, I draw upon writers who are geared towards a slightly younger audience. Throughout lockdown this meant that the children were still able to listen to Christian music and often could join in with actions.

3 **Bible verse of the week**
   At the same time as announcing the song of the week, I share the Bible verse of the week, which I try to keep as simple as possible. Children are given a merit (our school's

award system) if they are able to tell me on demand what the Bible verse is, which is a great incentive! The verse again ties in with the theme for that week, and I print it out and put it on my noticeboard.

4 **Assembly or chapel service**
This is obviously the main way to communicate the theme for the week. The thought for the week video sets it up, and then later in the week I get to do an all-age service or assembly, depending on the year group I'm seeing.

Visually, I really like having an ongoing prop I can develop; for example, I used a treasure chest for a whole term as I worked through Jesus' 'I am' statements from the Gospel of John. Each week we added another item to the chest, so that we could recall these aspects of Jesus that we can treasure. By the end, the chest was full. We had a fluffy sheep ('I am the good shepherd', John 10.11, 14), a loaf of bread—stale by now! ('the bread of life', John 6.35), a bunch of plastic grapes ('the vine', John 15.1), a torch ('light of the world', John 8.12) and so on. It was a useful way to help the children memorise what we'd been learning, and each week they were excited to see what new item would be joining the treasure chest.

Another term, we looked at the fruits of the Spirit. In a similar way, each week a new fruit was added to a bowl, representing a spiritual fruit. The peach of peace, guava of goodness and kiwi of kindness will not be forgotten in a hurry!

5 **Form-based activity**
From time to time I also have the opportunity to create a form-based activity to further help to expand on the theme. For example, during Advent I encouraged all the children to create in their classes a kindness Advent calendar, with

an act of kindness for each day in Advent; another time, they did a hot-seating drama activity to imagine what it would have been like to be Daniel or the lion in the Bible story. I think it's so important that Christianity isn't just talked about in gathered worship but that we find as many ways as possible to bring God into the normal school day.

Alongside these specific features of the school week, I give every classroom a prayer folder and ask the form teachers to read a short prayer (or ask a member of the class to choose a prayer) at the start of each day after taking the register. Each term I give them a selection of prayers for that season, and obviously it only takes a minute to begin the day in prayer but it's a moment for the class to collectively stop and remember to commit the day ahead into God's hands. In these small ways, school can really reinforce what is being taught and practised at home and in church, and vice versa.

It's amazing the power that a well-planned theme can have, not only for children but also for teachers and parents, when it's communicated through all these difference channels.

Early on in my chaplaincy I led a service about gratitude. Drawing on the story of the ten lepers, I spoke to the children about the importance and power of remembering to say thank you to God. I talked about worship as being an important way we thank God collectively for his goodness and love, and I drew comparison with singing 'Happy Birthday' to someone we love: a moment where voices unite to celebrate that person and their life and to show our love and appreciation for them.

It was a beautiful service, but what took me by surprise was the response I got from one of the parents several days later. This particular school mum, who wasn't a Christian, had been coming to chapel services for years, wanting to support her daughter. She had been shopping in London that weekend, just after visiting chapel, and the sun was bright and warm that particular day. She told me that suddenly the words of my talk had come into her mind, and for the first time in her parenting history she had stopped in her tracks and told her daughters they all needed to say thank you to God for the beautiful day and for all they had. She had told them that they all needed to be grateful. She slightly scrambled to explain to me what had happened in that moment, but I felt sure the Holy Spirit had been doing a work in her heart. Something had stirred within her in chapel the day before, and she had found herself wanting to respond to her Creator. This is the wonderful power of God when all ages gather. You never know whom God is going to speak to! I tend to have in the forefront of my mind the hundreds of children in front of me when I speak in my school context, but so often it's one of the grown-ups whom God seems to touch. I'm sure he's sowing seeds in the children's hearts all around the room, but also taking every chance he can to speak to the older ones, as this might be one of the very few times he's got their attention. If you're working in a school, the parents and teachers you come into contact with are also people whom God desperately wants to touch, so I encourage you to pray in faith and shine your light that all may see Jesus in you and come to know him for themselves.

I am a city on a hill
I am a light in the darkness
Jesus living in me can change the world
Let my light shine, let my light shine, let my light shine.

Extract from 'City on a Hill', by Nick and Becky Drake[1]

13
Next steps

There are two ways we tend to get motivated to act. The first is by seeing the need right in front of us. The alternative is by lifting our eyes and seeing a recurring pattern of need on a bigger scale. A lot of this book has been focussed on your local situation—your church, your people, your community—and we know that it can often feel like right there in front of your eyes is enough need to keep you active and motivated for a long time to come! But unfortunately, in the area of children and young people, it is when we lift our eyes to the wider context that the challenge becomes really sharp, the costs of inaction really high.

Children and young people in church

By 2018, here in the UK, the average number of children under sixteen who attended church (Church of England) on Sundays had dropped below 100,000 for the first time ever—'a new stage' had been reached.[1] Even worse, this number is declining each year at almost twice the rate of adult average Sunday attendance. By 2019, the number sat at around 89,700.[2] In Birmingham, for example, the second biggest city in the UK and the youngest city in Europe,[3] there is an average of only eleven children attending each church in the diocese (184 churches).

The statistics are shocking and impress upon us the urgency of the need to take action, and there are many working hard to change this outlook for children and young people in the church.[4] The reality is there is no simple, quick solution to the challenge. However, what is clear is that there is a huge need for new, *different* ways of 'doing' church to what has been the 'standard model' of worship up to now. Intergenerational worship, with the vision for belonging, participation and spirit-filled life outlined in this book, must be a key part of the road map ahead.

If the challenge is huge, so is the opportunity. The current generation of children (sixteen and under in 2021) are, for the first time, 'nonchurched' rather than unchurched. What that means is, 'They do not have the same cultural understanding and baggage in relation to church and what it means to be a Christian.'[5]

How can we reimagine church for this generation? If 56 per cent of Christians come to faith before they are ten and 75 per cent by eighteen[6]—what *intergenerational action* do we urgently need to take to encourage, foster and preserve a passing on 'from generation to generation' the experience of life with God and the wonder of knowing and worshipping him?

So what now?

One of the dangers of statistics like this and a book like this ironically is *inaction*. We can feel so overwhelmed by all there is to do that we park the things we have read and learnt and put off any action to another day that sometimes never comes. Alternatively, we close the book and desire to make a difference but just don't know where to start or what to do next. The crucial thing when you end this book is to commit to doing *the one next step*. Some of you will, of course, be called to make an impact on a big scale, but for most, the key question is: what is the *one thing* to do next in *your* context?

It could be that you're **in the congregation**, you're interested in this area, but you don't feel you have much gifting or influence to change things. Start by praying regularly. This is God's work and God's initiative, and you are called to partner with him. Ask him for guidance and an opportunity to speak to those who have influence. And in the meantime, how about you just begin leading where you can? Get to know someone from a different generation. Invite a family to lunch or have coffee with an older person. Start investing in intergenerational relationships.

It could be that you're **a young person** who's part of a church, you've got lots of ideas, but you feel you're never listened to. Again, start by praying! Pray for a mentor or older Christian to talk to. What are your gifts? Passions? Is there a way you could bring this to the church? Could you offer to serve on a rota? Or could you ask to shadow someone already serving in an area of ministry? Lead and serve where you can, and pray that God will use you to influence the culture in your community.

It could be that you work in **children or youth ministry**. You are perfectly positioned to both inspire and lead change in this area. Starting with where you are right now, how can your current ministry systems and structures lend themselves to more intergenerational overlap? Could your children and youth be brought more into the main worship? Could older generations be invited into children's groups to share and serve? Do you need to get this book into the hands of your church leader? If you are someone who regularly addresses the congregation during all-age worship, can you begin to articulate a vision for intergenerational worship?

It could be that you are **a church leader**. Looking at your current set-up, you might be pleased with how you're doing! Or perhaps your brain is now buzzing with things you want to develop or change. Is it time to start building a team who can pray and pioneer change with you? Are there key people whom even today you could call and start the conversation? What do you sense God is saying to you going forward? You are the one who will set the vision and the culture for intergenerational change. You're not on your own—God is with you.

As you've read through the various chapters of this book, we've created several moments to pause and reflect, to think through a series of questions that we've crafted to help you apply what you've learnt to your context. Unless you've been a particularly diligent student and made notes, it's likely you've already forgotten some of the questions and answers you've pondered on!

Don't worry. One of our prayers and key goals is that this book isn't merely about giving information but leads to a transformation of heart. What has shifted within you as you've journeyed with us through these pages? Our hope is that at a foundational level, you've been awakened to the need to become more and more intergenerational as a church, and the power of it. From that place, much of what has to happen is for you in your context, hand in hand with God, to pray and work out your next steps. There's no rulebook or one set of solutions, but we hope that we've given you some ideas and help in moving forward.

If we were to summarise where you go from here, this would be our list:

1 Pray

2 Gather a team

3 Talk about and share your vision and values for intergenerational worship. You can use our chapter on vision to help with this.

4 Look at the various components of your current worship and church life and be honest about where change needs to happen. You can refer back to the questions at the end of each chapter for help with this.

5 Decide where you'll make your first change.

6 And then go for your second. One step at a time.

7 Keep praying. Expect setbacks, but keep going! Unity across generational barriers is on God's heart, and God's power is at work in and through you as you serve.

We hope you feel encouraged. We hope you feel inspired. And we pray that each of you reading will feel equipped and motivated to play your part in bringing the generations together, so we can grow together, learn from one another and reflect more fully the image of our glorious Creator and loving Father. The Father of us all. That's you and you and you and you. The big family of God.

APPENDICES

Appendix 1: Sample all-age talks

For some of us, crafting an all-age talk will come very naturally, but for others it's still a real challenge. Hopefully the tips we've given will be helpful, but in this section we have transcribed some talks we have given in intergenerational services, to help show the structure and content.

1 Christmas talk: LIGHT

We've got four children, and our littlest is called Levi Emmanuel Drake *(baby picture of him on the screen)*. When we named him, we loved each of the names and also loved the fact that if you take all the initials, L. E. D., it reminds us that he is our little LIGHT! An LED light!

At Christmas time there are lights everywhere, aren't there? Fairy lights on the tree, lights in our windows, lights switched on in our streets. Everywhere we go, little lights shine in the darkness. And this is a great reminder of the greatest light of all—Jesus, the light of the world.

But why is Jesus described as the light of the world in the Bible? Well, I've brought a few little clues with me today—could I have four volunteers?

Bring volunteers to the front and give each of them a stocking.

Inside your stockings are some clues that can help us to understand why Jesus is described as a light. Let's open the first one.

Stocking one: a torch

Let's turn the torch on! Flash it around! A torch helps us to see in the darkness. It helps to give us direction and show us what's

132

ahead of us. In the same way, Jesus came to bring direction and help us to see in the darkness. He showed us the face of God! He showed us what the future would be like! He was like a torch.

Stocking two: a light bulb

Light bulbs are everywhere! They're a normal part of daily life. In the winter, they're the first thing we put on in the morning and the last thing we turn off at night. If we step outside, bulbs light up our street lamps. If we go inside, every room in every building has a light bulb. Jesus is like a light bulb because his presence is with us every day, everywhere we go. His light goes with us.

Stocking three: a lightsabre

Wow! A lightsabre! Let's turn it on and move it around! Are there any *Star Wars* fans here today? You'll know that a lightsabre is POWERFUL! It is a weapon that defeats darkness. In the same way, Jesus, the light of the world, came into the world to expose darkness and fight it! He came to show what was wrong and unjust, and to shine a light on the earth and bring healing and a new way of living. So Jesus' light is a powerful light!

Stocking four: glowsticks

Finally, let's crack some glowsticks together. You'll see now that some of our team are bringing around glowsticks for each of you. That's because as well as all these other forms of light, the glowstick helps us to remember that light is fun! And Jesus is fun! Jesus came to bring life to the full, so Christmas is a time to celebrate! Think of fireworks, birthday cake candles and fairy lights! They all remind us of parties and celebrations.

And that's what we're going to do now. As we worship together, let's wave our glowsticks and celebrate Jesus, the light of the world. Unlike the torch and lightsabre, whose batteries will eventually run out, or the light bulb, which will stop working, or the glowsticks, which won't glow tomorrow, Jesus' light will last FOREVER! He is the everlasting light—and that's a great reason to party!

Music can play—'Every Eye Is on You' or 'Hear the Bells Ringing'—as the congregation wave their glowsticks.

Analysis

To briefly analyse the 'light' talk, it opens with a personal story about our youngest child, immediately grabbing everyone's attention, and the visual picture also helps to engage the youngest.

Then very soon, there is participation from the congregation as volunteers come to the front. This keeps up the energy and adds interest for those watching.

The stockings bring an element of surprise and interest for everyone. The images of light help to explain Jesus as the light of the world, while breaking up the teaching with fun and engaging visual props.

The glowsticks bring participation to everyone and lead into praise and joy to end the talk.

2 **Easter talk: a tick or a cross?**

Hold up a big green tick. I cut one out of a cardboard box and painted it.

We all like to see one of these, don't we? When we get a tick at the end of our work, how does it make us feel? That's right, we feel pleased, happy, successful. We know we've done a good job and got our work right.

Now hold up a red cross.

But how do we feel when this appears at the end of our work? Maybe disappointed? A bit sad? It's never nice thinking we've made a mistake, especially when we've worked hard and tried our best.

So often a cross makes us think of failure. It can make us feel pretty bad.

And of course that's how Jesus' friends must have felt on Good Friday, when they stood before the cross and saw it as a place of death.

But let's think for a moment where else we might see a cross like this. Does anyone have any ideas?

You can take ideas from the people—they may say the following. If not, you can make these points:

1 **TREASURE!** That's right—X marks the spot! *(If you have a treasure chest you could hold it up, or put an image of a treasure chest on the screen.)* A cross reminds us of gold that pirates hunt for! And in the same way, the cross of Jesus was greater than gold. It brought us new life and brought us back to God, which is the greatest treasure we could ever find.

2 **A KISS!** When we write a card or a letter to someone we love, we sign off with a kiss. *(Image of greeting card on the screen.)* It's a sign of love. And in the same way, the cross of Jesus was a cross of love—the greatest act of love possible.

Jesus' death on the cross brought us back into relationship with our Father God. The Bible tells us that God so loved the world that he gave his only son, that whoever believes in him will not perish but will have everlasting life. So this act of love has bought us eternal life!

3 **X FACTOR!** Are there any *X Factor* fans here? *(Put a picture from the show on the screen.)* If you have the X factor, it means you have something very special and unique. Well, the cross of Jesus reminds us that Jesus is the most special and unique man who ever walked this earth! He takes the X factor to a whole new level! He's the King of all kings, and the very best friend we can ever have.

So, when we looked at the cross on Good Friday, it was easy to think that something had gone horribly wrong, like a big red cross under our work. This is how the disciples felt. But Easter Sunday shows us a whole other way of looking at the cross! This cross was a place of love, and a place of great treasure! It was a place that revealed the most special person who ever walked this earth. The cross is not a symbol of failure, but it's actually a huge TICK over all of our lives! *(Hold the tick up again.)*

Analysis

In this talk, immediately the tick and cross and interactive questions give a visual aid and talking point to the congregation.

Following on from this, there is further engagement as the people give suggestions of where they may have seen the cross symbol. This is further supported by any images you can display on the screen.

Returning to the tick at the end brings a nice completion to the image and provides an opportunity to teach and reinforce the amazing power of the Easter message.

3 **God speaks through creation!**

This talk would follow the theme of creation and specifically God speaking through creation. At some point in the service preceding the talk, Psalm 19 needs to be read.

I'd like to start by asking for a volunteer to help me! *(Pick someone who will be able to draw—the images don't need to be brilliant but do have to be recognisable, so preferably find someone aged eight or older. For the sake of this talk, we have named our volunteer Maya.)*

I thought it would be really nice if we could get to know Maya today, so in a minute I'm going to see if any of you would like to ask Maya a question about herself. BUT, Maya isn't allowed to speak—instead, she has to DRAW her answers. *(Give Maya a large sheet of paper and several pens.)*

Now, I'm going to start us off and then I will come to the floor. Maya, could you start by drawing how old you are? Then could you tell us how you're feeling today?

Take other questions. You can encourage people to ask what her favourite things are, such as favourite colour, favourite food, best school subject, etc.

OK, thank you, Maya! Now before you sit down, let's see if we can all guess your answers together. *(Go through the list one by one, saying 'So, Maya is eleven! Maya likes the colour yellow', etc.)*

Now, Maya hasn't said a word, but we have been able to get to know her through what she has created. It's no different with God. He has painted and sculpted creation in such a way that it speaks of him and we can get to know him more through looking at the world around us.

Put Psalm 19.1 on the screen, or read it again.

This verse tells us that the heavens declare the glory of God! The skies are speaking to us of God's greatness!

How about these images? How do we see God through them?

*You could show a mountain, displaying God's strength
    and might.*
*You could show the sea, speaking of the width and depth
    of God's love.*
A flower or bumblebee might show God's artistry or gentleness.
*A picture of a baby or several faces will show something
    of God's own face—we are made in his image.*

When we get outside and into creation, if we pray and look for it, there are signs of God all around us, and he wants to reveal more of himself through creation. In fact, Jesus said in Luke 19, verse 40, that if the people stay silent, 'the stones will cry out in praise'!

So, as we respond together now, let's take a moment to watch this beautiful video, and ask God to stir up praise and wonder in our hearts as we think of him and his amazing creation!

There are several videos on YouTube, such as Brian Doerksen's 'Creation Calls' and Hillsong's 'So Will I', that work very well at this point for a reflective end. Our song 'Creator God' works well as a more joyful closing.

Analysis

The talk begins by using a volunteer and is interactive, which immediately involves the congregation. All ages can get involved in this and will enjoy interpreting the drawings. The central metaphor that comes from this is clever but also accessible, and we have found that all ages have really engaged with this concept. It's a very gentle way in to listening to God, as all can feel comfortable getting outside and looking for signs of God in creation. I've used this as the opening of a series on listening to the voice of God, moving on to 'God speaks through the Bible', 'God speaks through us, 'God speaks through dreams' and 'God speaks in words and pictures/prophetically'.

Appendix 2: A sample service plan and script

The following script was referred to in Chapter 10. It gives an example of how drama might be used in a service to open up or develop a theme.

SHOW-AND-TELL

Cast

   Teacher
   Polly
   Bertie
   Ryan
   Rosie
   Barnaby

Slightly eccentric teacher walks out and addresses the class.

Teacher (*facing congregation*): Morning, class! OK, OK, Oliver, please take your pencil out of Reuben's ear! Jemima! JE-MI-MA! WAKE UP! Thank you! What is it, Jimmy? You've lost your PE kit? Wait a minute . . . FOR GOODNESS SAKE, Lily, sit down and stop pretending to be Lady Gaga.

Right!
So it's that time in the week where you all bring in your (*sarcastically*) fascinating little random things to school . . . Yes, it's time for SHOW-AND-TELL!
So, first up—come on, Polly, what have you brought to school today? (*One by one, children come on stage.*)

Polly: A sock.

Teacher: A sock?

Polly: It belonged to my grandpa. I love it. It's got a hole in the big toe.

Teacher: Thank you. *(Confused pause.)* Right, Bertie, your turn—what have you got?

Bertie *(class nerd in glasses)*: I have brought the *Oxford Encyclopaedia of Worms*.

Teacher: Of words?

Bertie: No, worms.

Teacher: The wriggly type?

Bertie: Well, the interesting thing is, sir, that not all worms wriggle in the way one might expect. For example—

Teacher *(puts hand up)*: No examples needed. Ryan! Come forward, what have you got today?

Ryan *(holding a covered box)*: MY PET SNAKE!

Teacher *(petrified, leaping on his chair)*: WHAT? Are you serious? Ryan, you are not allowed living, breathing creatures in this school! Get out! I mean ... *(Coughs and composes himself. Continues slowly:)* I mean, will you please go immediately to Mrs Walker in the office and tell her to call your mother straight away so she can come and collect your pet snake. Billy, go with him, please. *(Sits down.)* NEXT! Come on, Rosie. *(Desperate:)* Tell me you've got something fascinating for us today?

Rosie: I have a very interesting ancient egg cup, sir.

Teacher (*relieved*): Ah! At last! Thank you, Rosie. Ancient? How wonderful—a bit of history! (*Eyes widening:*) How ancient is it?

Rosie: I left the egg in it for three whole months and it's very, very hairy and very, very mouldy. Do you want to look more closely, sir?

Teacher (*quickly*): NO! No—no thank you, Rosie. You and your mouldy egg may sit down.

(*Sighs.*)

Well, it looks like we have time for just one more. (*Commotion from the class.*) Yes, I know, I know! You all want to have a go! There'll be more next week. Now let me see, who might possibly have something good to show and tell . . . hmmmmm . . . Barnaby Tucker. How about you? Come forward!

(*Barnaby walks slowly forward.*)

Teacher: Well? Barnaby? What have you brought? Oh, please don't tell me you've forgotten.

Barnaby: No sir, I've not forgotten.

Teacher: Well, where is it? What have you brought to show-and-tell?

Barnaby: Me.

(*Teacher pauses and looks quizzical . . . then puts head on table in despair.*)

Appendix 3: Suggested songs by theme

For easy reference, we have listed our Worship for Everyone songs thematically for specific occasions or times of worship. Each of these songs can be found on our website at www. worshipforeveryone.com. Lyric videos can be viewed via our YouTube channel or downloaded directly from our website for use in schools and churches.

Opening praise
Out of the Water
God Is Good
Creator God
Big Family of God
Every Eye Is on You
God Is Here
The Singing Song

God as Father
Creator God
I Am His child
Father
God Is Love
God Is Good
When You Are Sleeping

Jesus-centred
The Rock
Sign Your Cross
City on a Hill

Our God's Generous
We Wanna Be Like Jesus
All Through History
Speak Your Name
Every Eye Is on You

Holy Spirit
Sign Your Cross
How Do I Know?

Faithfulness and hope
The Rock
All through History
Faith
Slingshot
The Ark
Every Step
My God Is Everywhere

Easter
Forever Yours
Out of the Water
Our God's Generous
Sign Your Cross
All through History

Harvest
Our God's Generous
Creator God

Christmas
The Angels Knew
Hear the Bells
Oh, What a Day!

Sending/closing songs

City on a Hill
Every Step
Big Family of God
Every Eye Is on You
The Ark
Faith

Creation

Creator God
Unique
That's How You Made Me

God's family

Big Family of God
Golden Rule Is Love
The Singing Song
God Is Love
God Is Good

Songs to encourage and strengthen

Slingshot
Speak Your Name
When You Are Sleeping
God Is Good
The Ark
Faith
I Am His Child
My God Is Everywhere
Unique
Father
When the Morning Comes

Notes

Introduction

1 For further reading and especially analysis of why the church has often colluded with this approach, see Allen, H.C., and Ross, C.L., *Intergenerational Christian Formation* (Downers Grove, IL, IVP Academic, 2012), pp. 35–44.

2 Tapper, J. 'How the Elderly Can Help the Young—and Help Themselves' (*The Guardian*, January 2019), https://www.theguardian.com/society/2019/jan/05/children-eldery-intergenerational-care-advantages. Such initiatives have been running in other parts of the world for a long time; see, for example, Newman, S., Ward, C.R., Smith, T.B., Wilson, J.O., McCrea, J.M., Calhoun, G., and Kingson, E., *Intergenerational Programs: Past, Present and Future* (Washington, DC, Taylor and Francis, 1997); Kuehne, V., *Intergenerational Programming: Understanding What We Have Created* (New York, Haworth Press, 1999).

3 For example, see Allen and Ross, *Intergenerational Christian Formation*, pp. 18–21, 64–74; cf. Allen, H.C., ed., *InterGenerate: Transforming Churches Through Intergenerational Ministry* (Abilene, TX, Abilene Christian University Press, 2018), pp. 17–24. One of the earliest proponents of this term was Gambone, J.V., *All Are Welcome: A Primer for Intentional Intergenerational Ministry and Dialogue* (Crystal Bay, MN, Elder Eye Press, 1998). Gambone proposed the need for 'intentional intergenerational ministry'.

4 For an example of classic church leadership advice along generational lines, see Rendle, G., *The Multigenerational Congregation: Meeting the Leadership Challenge* (Bethesda, MD, Alban Institute, 2002).

5 Drake, N., and Drake, B., 'Faith' (*All Through History: 10 Years of Worship for Everyone*, Daybreak Music/Elevation, 2018), www.songsolutions.org.

2 Forming a vision for all-age worship?

1 Eph. 5.8: The word translated 'enlightened' is actually present continuous—not a one-off, but continuously switched on in the realm of faith.

2 Verse 17 could be paraphrased: 'May you grasp what the Spirit desires to give you'—specifically, *sophia*, wisdom for practical living, and *apocalypses*, revelation—insight into God's plans and purposes. So, wisdom for practical living and insight into God's plans and purposes—the day-to-day and the long range.

3 If I want to meet a friend for a relaxed chat with 'happy' (sweetened) coffee, I'd probably choose the Starbucks experience—softer chairs, brighter yet relaxed visuals, more 'fun' drinks to mess with!

4 And see Chapter 5 for what makes intergenerational ministry hard.

5 Drake, B., and Drake, N.J., 'Every Step'. Worship for Everyone 2018, www.songsolutions.org.

6 This is a phrase that has begun to be used a lot, and yet its original source seems unclear. We first heard it from our friend Lynn Alexander in the late 2000s. See her book: Alexander, L., *Children, Families and God: Drawing the Generations Together to Change the World* (Destiny Image Europe/Evangelista Media 2012).

7 'Sing to him a new song; play skilfully, and shout for joy.' NIV.

8 Lewis, C.S., 'On Three Ways of Writing for Children' (*On Stories, and Other Essays on Literature*, Harvest Books, 2002).

3 A theology of Worship for Everyone: Old Testament

1 St Paul's Theological College Malaysia, https://www.sptc.my.

2 A good introduction drawing on various sources is Alexander, *Children, Families and God*. A more detailed collection of studies can be found in Hess, R.S., and Carroll R., M.D., *Family in the Bible* (Grand Rapids, MI, Baker Academic, 2003).

3 See throughout the Psalms—e.g. Pss. 71, 78, 100, 102, 119, 145.

4 The Jewish confession of faith, called the *Shema*—see Andrews, J., 'Who We Worship: The Lord Who Is One' (*Why Worship*, Hughes, T., Drake, N., Hoeksma, L., eds, London, SPCK, 2021).

5 See Kirk, D., *Heirs Together: Establishing Intergenerational Church* (Buxhall, Kevin Mayhew, 2003).

6 Wenham, G., 'Family in the Pentateuch' (*Family in the Bible*, Hess, R.S., and Carroll M.D., Grand Rapids, MI, Baker Academic, 2003), pp. 20–21.

7 See, for example, Sánchez, E., 'Family in the Non-narrative Sections of the Pentateuch' (*Family in the Bible*, Hess, R.S., and Carroll M.D., Grand Rapids, MI, Baker Academic, 2003), pp. 32–36.

8 See Stager, L.E., 'The Archaeology of the Family in Ancient Israel' (*Bulletin of the American Schools of Oriental Research* 260 1985), pp. 11–24.

9 See Meyers, C.L., 'The Family in Early Israel' (*Families in Ancient Israel*, Perdue, L.G., Blenkinsopp, J., Collins, J.J., and Meyers, C.L., Louisville, KY, Westminster John Knox, 1997). There are also references to *bêt ʾem*, the 'mother's house', but this tends to be used to express a special tie to the mother for an unmarried woman, such as Rebekah in Genesis 24.28. Tsumura argues this unit would still be seen as part of the wider *bêt ʾāb*. See Tsumura, D.T., 'Family in the Historical Books' (*Family in the Bible*, Hess, R.S., and Carroll M.D., Grand Rapids, MI, Baker Academic, 2003), pp. 59–79.

10 See also what happens when the Lord calls out his sin in v.4–15. For more on these categories and this passage, see a good commentary such as Hess, R.S., *Joshua: An Introduction and Commentary*, Tyndale Old Testament Commentaries (Downers Grove, IL, InterVarsity, 1996), pp. 150–51.

11 Wenham, 'Family in the Pentateuch', p. 21.

12 Beginning with Moltmann, J., *The Trinity and the Kingdom of God* (San Francisco, CA, Harper & Row, 1981). For implications for church, see Volf, M., *After Our Likeness: The Church as an Image of the Trinity* (Grand Rapids, MI,

Eerdmans, 1998). The watershed text perhaps is Zizioulas, J.D., *Being as Communion: Studies in Personhood and the Church* (London, DLT, 1985).

13 Thanks to Lynn Alexander for first drawing our attention to this aspect of the story in conversation and in *Children, Families and God*.

14 Alexander, *Children, Families and God*, p. 62 (Kindle location 944).

4 A theology of Worship for Everyone: New Testament

1 Again, it is important to note this isn't a comprehensive review of the material and there is more to be explored. An interesting introduction to this topic in general is Richards, A., *Children in the Bible* (London, SPCK, 2013). For an academic collection of essays, see Bunge, M., ed., *The Child in the Bible* (Grand Rapids, MI, Eerdmans, 2008).

2 Space prevents here a discussion of the Pauline material, in which children are used instead to symbolise the early stages of the journey of following in the way of Jesus (1 Cor. 13.11; 14.20; James 1.6; Heb. 5.13; 1 Peter 2.2).

3 D.A. Hagner writes, 'The social insignificance, if not the innocent unself-consciousness of the little child, was the very antithesis of the disciples' interest in power and greatness.' *Word Biblical Commentary,* vol. 33B: Matthew 14–28 (Dallas, TX, Word, 1995), p. 517.

4 Aasgaard, R. *My Beloved Brothers and Sisters: Christian Siblingship in Paul* (Edinburgh, UK, T&T Clark, 2004), p. 38.

5 Stark, R., *The Rise of Christianity* (San Francisco, CA, Harper Collins, SanFrancisco, 1997), p. 92.

6 Westfall, C.L., 'Family in the Gospels and Acts' (*Family in the Bible*, Hess, R.S., and Carroll M.D., Grand Rapids, MI, Baker Academic, 2003), pp. 125–247.

7 Richards, *Children in the Bible*, p. 103.

8 Ibid.

9 Alexander, *Children, Families and God*, p. 97 (Kindle location 1540).

10 Rodney Stark, in his exploration of the rise of Christianity in the generations following Jesus, concludes that the church's treatment of children was one of the key reasons for its success. Stark, R., *The Rise of Christianity* (San Francisco, CA, Harper Collins, 1997), pp. 97, 128.

11 Westfall, C.L., 'Family in the Gospels and Acts' (*Family in the Bible*, Hess, R.S., and Carroll M.D., Grand Rapids, MI, Baker Academic, 2003), p. 128.

12 There are differing perspectives on the importance of family in Jesus' teaching, e.g. Luke 11.27–8; Mark 3.31–5; Luke 14.12–14. For discussion see Westfall, pp. 134–5 in Hess and Carroll, who writes, 'When Jesus chose his disciples and taught them and the crowds about discipleship, he relativized the priority of family without being antifamily' (p. 134). See also Ellis, I., 'Jesus and the Subversive Family' (*Scottish Journal of Theology* 38, 1985), pp. 173–88; Barton, S.C., *Discipleship and Family Ties in Mark and Matthew*, Society for New Testament

Studies Monograph Series 80 (Cambridge, UK, Cambridge University Press. 1994), pp. 23–56.

13 Jesus starts this language by describing those who follow him in familial terms (Matt 12.46–50; 28.10; Mark 3.31–5; Luke 8.19–21; John 20.17).

14 BBC, 'Boy, 5, Invites Entire Class to Watch His Adoption' (BBC News, December 2019), https://www.bbc.co.uk/news/world-us-canada-50683948.

15 For more, see Aasgaard, *My Beloved Brothers and Sisters.*

16 See also, for example, Gal. 3.23–9; 4.4–7.

17 The word *sonship* here (NIV) meaning followers of Jesus who are transformed legally to be 'heirs' of God.

18 Calvin, J., *Institutes of the Christian Religion* (1536), 3.20.37.

19 Drake, N., and Drake, B., 'Big Family of God' (*All Through History: 10 Years of Worship for Everyone*, Daybreak Music/Elevation, 2018), www.songsolutions.org.

20 Drake, N., and Drake, B., 'God Is Good'. Integrity Music Europe, 2020.

21 See, for example, the reading by Ernest Best; Best, E., *Ephesians* (Edinburgh, UK, T&T Clark, 1998), p. 344. Unfortunately there isn't space here to discuss in detail the metaphor of the body in Paul's writing, such as in 1 Cor. 12.12, but there is much fruit to be found in building foundations on that imagery for intergenerational worship too.

22 I have written elsewhere about this; see https://bham
.academia.edu/nickjdrake.

5 What makes all-age worship so difficult?

1 This is where ministry is divided up according to generational
or stage-of-life categories and therefore targets people in
groups accordingly.

6 What do children need?

1 After physical and safety needs are met, this is the most
important need for all of us, according to the classic
'hierarchy of needs' by psychologist Abraham Maslow
(Maslow, A., *Motivation and Personality*. New York, Harper
& Brothers, 1954).

2 In *Children in the Bible*, Anne Richards shares a story that
(unfortunately) illustrates this brilliantly. The vicar's wife,
known as 'The Shadow', would appear at the side of a parent
during the sermon and remove without a word any child or
baby who was distracting her husband, the vicar, from his
sermon! See p. 80.

3 Turner, R., *Parenting Children for a Life of Purpose* (Abingdon,
UK, BRF, 2014).

4 Armstrong, L., *Children in Worship: The Road to Faith*
(Melbourne, Australia, Joint Board of Christian Education,
1988).

5 Beckwith, I., *Postmodern Children's Ministry: Ministry to
Children in the 21st Century Church* (Grand Rapids, MI,
Zondervan, 2004), p. 66.

7 Using songs in all-age worship

1 Drake, N., and Drake, B., 'The Singing Song'. Thankyou Music, 2011.

2 Drake, N., and Drake, B., 'Creator God' (*All Through History: 10 Years of Worship for Everyone*, Daybreak Music/Elevation, 2018), www.songsolutions.org.

3 You can listen to the songs mentioned in this chapter and more on our YouTube channel, youtube.com/worshipforeveryone, or on Spotify, iTunes, Amazon Music and other music services. Resources are available at www.worshipforeveryone.com.

4 Drake, N., and Drake, B., 'All Through History' (*All Through History: 10 Years of Worship for Everyone*, Daybreak Music/Elevation, 2018), www.songsolutions.org.

5 King Of My Heart by John and Sarah McMillan. © 2015 Jesus Culture Music, under exclusive license to Sparrow Records.

10 Constructing an all-age service

1 We're aware every context will be different. Some of you will have structures based on liturgy, some will be totally free. But most of these principles can be adapted across different traditions.

2 See Chapter 2, on vision and values.

3 Lloyd-Jones, S., *The Jesus Storybook Bible: Every Story Whispers His Name* (Grand Rapids, MI, Zondervan, 2007).

4 Find this song and others by subscribing to our YouTube channel, youtube.com/worshipforeveryone, or following us on any online music service.

12 Worship for schools

1 Drake, N., and Drake, B., 'City on a Hill' (Thankyou Music, 2014; *All Through History: 10 Years of Worship for Everyone*, Daybreak Music/Elevation, 2018), www.songsolutions.org.

13 Next steps

1 Paper, 'Children and Youth Ministry' to the General Synod *(GS 2161)*, February 2020. This was based on an assessment of children and young people's Sunday attendance over a five-year period from 2014–2018. The full research can be found here: https://www.churchofengland.org/sites /default/files/2020-01/GS%202161%20Children%20and%20 Youth%20Ministry%20Full%20with%20Appendix%20-%20 Final.pdf

2 Thirteen per cent of a total of 854,000 average attendance. *Statistics for Mission 2019* (Research and Statistics, 2020). This document is available online at https:// www.churchofengland.org/sites/default/files/2020 -10/2019StatisticsForMission.pdf.

3 Nearly 40 per cent of the population is under twenty-five. See Harris, C., 'People' (*The Birmingham Economic Review 2018*, City-REDI/University of Birmingham/Greater Birmingham Chambers of Commerce 2019), https://blog.bham.ac.uk /cityredi/the-birmingham-economic-review-2018-people -population-and-employment.

4 For example, the Capital Youth program in London, Birmingham's 'Transforming Church: Growing Younger' and Southwell and Nottingham's 'Wider, Younger, Deeper' focus. For more research on teenage engagement in the church in particular, see the excellent work done by Youthscape: https://www.youthscape.co.uk/research.

5 'Children and Youth Ministry' to the General Synod.

6 Methodology • Com. Res, 'Mapping Practising Christians'. 2017. For this study, 8,150 UK adults were interviewed.